That Girl with Cancer

BRIANNE DISHONG

That Girl with Cancer

TATE PUBLISHING
AND ENTERPRISES, LLC

That Girl with Cancer
Copyright © 2014 by Brianne Dishong. All rights reserved.

No part of this publication may be reproduced, stored in a retrieval system or transmitted in any way by any means, electronic, mechanical, photocopy, recording or otherwise without the prior permission of the author except as provided by USA copyright law.

The opinions expressed by the author are not necessarily those of Tate Publishing, LLC.

Published by Tate Publishing & Enterprises, LLC
127 E. Trade Center Terrace | Mustang, Oklahoma 73064 USA
1.888.361.9473 | www.tatepublishing.com

Tate Publishing is committed to excellence in the publishing industry. The company reflects the philosophy established by the founders, based on Psalm 68:11,
"The Lord gave the word and great was the company of those who published it."

Book design copyright © 2014 by Tate Publishing, LLC. All rights reserved.
Cover design by Junriel Boquecosa
Interior design by Jake Muelle

Published in the United States of America

ISBN: 978-1-62854-212-7
1. Biography & Autobiography / Medical
2. Medical / Oncology
13.12.16

Dedication

This book is dedicated to all of those who believed in me and fought with me, to all of my friends, family, and those friends who became family.

Especially dedicated to my best friends in this world, Mom and Dad. Your support and strength carried me through this entire battle.

And to those fighting: Keep your spirits up and your faith strong. Keep Fighting.

Acknowledgments

Thanking everyone who helped me survive is nearly impossible. I had the biggest and greatest support team imaginable and it started from the moment the news of my diagnosis had spread.

The community of Stow was incredible to me. And showed me that once you are a Bulldog you will always be a Bulldog. The support my town gave to not just myself but also my family was overwhelming and greatly appreciated. I have never been more proud to be a part of our community, and I hope to always make the town proud.

It is also very important to me to acknowledge Slippery Rock University. From my friends to my professors, there wasn't a moment that I couldn't feel the support coming from my school. Specifically I have to thank my lacrosse team, who never made me feel like I was a cancer patient. The team gave me something to look forward to on hard days and so much to be proud of every time they took the field wearing my number on their back.

One of the most incredible support groups I had came from the summer camp I work at. These people that I see for two months out of the year were amazing to me. Camp was always my finish line. I had to be done fighting to get to camp and the fact that the directors allowed me to do so is something I will never be able to thank them enough for. My camp "crew," the division heads, and the campers, I am not sure that I have told you what you all did for me in that summer, but you gave a bald, eyebrow-less woman more strength than you know. To the campers reading this: you all need to know how incredible you are. You made me feel like the most beautiful person to walk the earth at a time when most kids would be afraid to be around someone. You all have the ability to do such great things in this world and you continually teach me something new about myself. Wherever life takes you please remember that I am always on your side.

To my family: I don't know how I would've gotten through this battle without all of you. Uncle Matt, you tell me that I am your hero at times, but I need you to know that you are mine. You saved me with your words on more than one occasion and you gave me strength when the visits from friends slowed down. I am so grateful for the time we spent together when I was sick and I am so glad to have you in my life.

I was fortunate to have so much support, but even more fortunate to have a friend like Lindsay. You were the reason I stayed sane. You were the only one I could really tell the truth to without fear. I know that it had to be hard for you to hear the things I was saying at times, but the way you handled it was exactly what I needed. There was not one time when you made me feel crazy for what I was feeling. You let me feel it and express it then you would help me rationalize. I will never forget the moment after my battle when you told me that I had my eyes again. I never even knew they were missing! I am not sure how you held on to those thoughts when you would see me. You and Mike will always be my family and I loved every minute spent with the two of you. Thank you both for taking me in when I visited school and for all the laughs we have together.

Now for the hardest thank you, Mom & Dad. I am not really sure where to start. You two are the reason I won this battle. From everything you taught me as a child, to all the support you gave to me in that chemo room. You raised me to be a fighter. You always made me work hard for the things I wanted. Even when Dad was my basketball coach you guys made me work ten times harder than everyone and every year I was afraid my own father would cut me from his team!! You never let me slip and you never let me do things half way. That is the reason I was strong enough to win. I never had a doubt in my mind that I could beat cancer because you raised me that way. I hope to be as great to my kids someday as you have been to me. Your faith and strength gets me through every day and I am beyond blessed to have you for parents. I always know I'll conquer whatever life throws my way because I have you two in my heart and on my team.

Contents

Is This Real Life? 13
Just Another Day 17
Spirits up. Faith strong. Body moving. 21
I Can Be Weak 25
A Little Bit Stronger 29
Cancer's Holiday Vacation. 33
Bald is Beautiful. Says My Bald Brother! 35
One step closer… 39
Nausea, Chest Pains, and Mouth Sores. Oh My!. 43
One Day at a Time. 47
Nothing Profound, Just Procrastination 51
What a Trip!. 55
The Sixth-Grade Boy Who Changed My Life 61
If Seeing is Believing… 67
Still I Rise, Still I Fight 71
This was Supposed to be My Week Away. 75
A Weekend to Remember 79
Another Day of Kryptonite Behind Me… 85

I'm Not lucky, I'm Blessed 87
Surgery, Stewart's, and Balding 91
Greatness 95
So Happy 99
Sunscreen, Gallon Challenge, and My Rocks 103
Fight. 107
Sorry! 113
Light… 117
Fourth Quarter 121
YOLO 125
So Close! 129
Victory. 133
Keep Fighting 137
Long Over Due Update 139
For the Last Time… 147
Bri's Quick Chemo Survival Guide 155

Is This Real Life?
12/08/2011

I have cancer. Holy crap, I have cancer! Is it weird that I'm not that surprised? I'll beat it; there is no question in my mind that I'll win, but really?

When the doctor said Lymphoma, here's what went through my mind: 1. There's absolutely no way I have cancer; it's got to be some other unexplainable medical phenomenon that only I could acquire. 2. I'll beat it. 3. How am I going to get my family through this? Mom is crying watching me sit on a table at the doctor's office! 4. I was finally getting my life organized, and now I have to slow those plans down.

I'm not scared really. Sure, it will be painful, and yeah I'm gonna wish I was having another knee surgery, but I'm not. At the age of twenty-two, I will be playing the biggest opponent of my life. I am an athlete. I am strong. I just graduated from a Division II University where my ultimate goal was shattered because I blew out my knee my senior year. I had said I'd give anything to compete again. I definitely didn't mean to challenge life, but I'll take it.

I'm not afraid of this disease. I'm not afraid to go toe to toe with this ugly beast inside of me and rip it out. I have my family, I have my friends, I have my team, and I have thousands of other survivors in my corner. So, *Cancer*, do what you want for now, make me tired, make me weak, try to bring me down. You won't last long. In fact, you are a complete joke. Can you hear me laughing? I don't give a crap about you. You can't stop me. Look at what I have overcome in my life, look at my support system, Good luck you sick bastard. I can't wait to be rid of you.

I remember waking up in the middle of October because my throat was killing me. Thinking that I must be getting a cold, I felt my neck to see if my lymph nodes were swollen, and when they were I wasn't surprised. Swollen lymph nodes were always common when I had a cold. I went back to bed and just figured I'd deal with it in the morning. I was a graduate assistant for the University lacrosse team that I played on through undergrad, I went to work just like any other day and told Lindsay, the assistant coach, to feel the huge lump in my neck. She told me to go to the health center and take care of myself, and we laughed as I called myself a freak. A couple of weeks later Lindsay and I were talking, and she yelled at me because she could actually see the lump on the left side of my neck. I of course told her to calm down; it was just a cold, after all.

About a month after I first discovered the lump, I was home for Thanksgiving break. My mom and I were watching movies, and I was running my hands through my long brown hair, I felt the lump. I simply said, "Oh, Mom, I've been meaning to show you this." The next day I was at the doctor's office, and the journey hadn't stopped since.

The first step of the diagnosis process was a needle biopsy. They use a CAT scan machine to assist with this and it is quite an experience. They set up a guide needle in the left side of my neck where I had found the lump, then they put me in the machine to make sure the needle is in the proper location. After that, they took me back out of the machine, and insert a needle within the guide and pull out a piece of the lymph node to biopsy. Just to make sure you're picturing this correctly, yes, I was in the machine with a needle sticking out of my neck, being held up by towels, and being told not to move. Totally normal, right? They do this process as many times as necessary in order to get results. I carried on many conversations with the nurses and technicians, but I only remember two. The first I can remember is that I had felt blood roll down the back of my neck. My reaction was to inform the nurse that if they didn't clean it well enough my mother would freak out on them! So, naturally when my parents walked in all the nurses asked my mom if she was ok. Her response; "Of course I'm ok! What about her?" Then the nurse proceeded to tell her that my only concern was that I was clean and healthy looking for my mom. The second memory of that biopsy was when the technician came in the room. I wanted to be prepared for any results, and I knew that they could tell from experience what cancer looks like. So, I asked him what he thought. He, of course, said he couldn't be sure until they received the results, but I pushed for more. He then informed me that in his experience I certainly had some form of cancer.

The form of cancer I would be taking on turned out to be Hodgkin's Lymphoma. My family and I braced ourselves and started the battle.

Just Another Day
12/15/2011

Yesterday I was at the Cleveland Clinic from six in the morning to six in the evening. What a great day! (Sarcasm). It started with some PET Scans and ended with more blood tests. I met my Lymphoma doctor, I actually have two, both with crazy accents. One asked my mom if she "appreciated the lump on my neck." WTF does that mean? *Haha* was my mom supposed to say "Oh I just loved it, felt *reeeal* nice, can she please have more?" Needless to say, we were all weary of that doctor at first. Then we met the second doctor and got to see all my scans; that was kind of cool actually; I like seeing what I'm dealing with. So, both sides of my neck have swollen lymph nodes, there are some in my left armpit, one big one in the middle of my chest, one near my heart, and all along my collar bone. What can I say when I do things, I do them right! Kidding. Actually, I am very lucky they stopped in my chest. So, the doctors believe I am at stage 2b, the *b* is just because I have night sweats and some other symptoms. They keep asking me about weight loss, and I mean there are a couple of pounds

I wouldn't mind losing, but I don't see that happening! They also need me to have surgery on the lump in my neck. They are 99% sure that the Hodgkin's diagnosis is correct but we want 100% here. So, on the 22nd I will go to a neck surgeon and be left with a little scar. The one request I had was that I didn't do a bone marrow biopsy. I mean, have you ever seen *My Sister's Keeper*? That crap looks painful! Of course I had to get one done so we took care of that yesterday too. The painkillers were worse than the procedure! I ended up getting sick from them, and just carried a conversation during the biopsy about dogs and what kind of drill they were using to get through my hip; I am so weird. Those results will come back on Monday, and if it shows that lymphoma is in my marrow, I go from stage 2 to stage 4, so prayers and fingers crossed for that to be negative! I found out a little about my treatment plan, and I am honestly not that worried about it. It will be hard, but life is hard. I remember giving advice to a camper who is in high school complaining about how they hate life and how hard it is, and I came up with what I thought was pretty good advice, so I saved what I said to her and I think it works now. I think she said she wished life were easy because my response was, "Nah, if life was easy it would be boring. Everyone would be weak and then when something challenging did happen, the world would crumble. Life's supposed to be hard and messy and imperfect. That's how it makes all the little things, the big things, and the good times that much better." Damn, I got deep there!

But here's to me loving and fighting for my hard, messy, imperfect life. And, I wouldn't have it any other way.

———

In college, I played Varsity Lacrosse at a Division II school in Pennsylvania. While competing, I helped build the program and continually improved on my personal statistics and accolades. Lacrosse was a huge part of my life, and I worked hard to be the player that I was. Within my career I had two knee surgeries; one was career ending. During my senior year, I was going for an interception in an away game and my leg gave out underneath me. I tore my ACL and meniscus, and ruined all plans of making my senior year the best of my career. I couldn't end hurt, and it was too late to red shirt, so my only option was to play on it. I took two weeks off to gain my strength and got back on the field. I never played the same again, but I had to do it. I had my surgery in August, so by November, when the cancer came to light, I was still trying to recover from the injury. That is why I took so long to speak up about the lump. My philosophy: If it isn't bleeding or falling off my body, it probably isn't a big deal. Well, obviously I was wrong.

Spirits up. Faith strong. Body moving.
12/18/2011

So, the waiting process sucks. As the hole in my back from the bone marrow is healing, I am still waiting for answers. The doctors told me the chances of the cancer being in my marrow are small and I didn't believe that it is there, but waiting for the results was driving me nuts. I had a dream last night that the results came back positive…didn't tell mom and dad about that but hey guys! Now ya know! Thanks for reading :)…Oh well though, it doesn't really matter what the results are, I'm still winning.

My grandparents are on their way home from Wyoming. I'm excited to see them, just wish they were coming home for different reasons. I know when grandma see's me it will be instant water works and I feel like if anyone can get me to cry it will be her! That's all right though, I realize crying is sometimes necessary. And don't get me wrong; I have had a couple of breakdowns. I just know that tears won't help me get better so I prefer to crack jokes. Speaking of jokes, I have a doctor appointment for my knee tomorrow. I am 22 going on 80, I swear! Hopefully the doc will tell me I can start running, but rehab has kind of taken a back seat since the diagnosis.

One of my only breakdowns so far was from the stress of just getting over a knee surgery. The injury broke my heart when it made my lacrosse career end in a way I never imagined and now getting diagnosed with cancer. When it rains it pours! My parents have been nervous that I will start asking *why me*? And, the day my family doctor said the word lymphoma, the question came to mind for about twenty seconds. Then I realized that I already have the answer: Because I can handle it. So, my breakdown of going from knee surgery to cancer wasn't a question of *why me*? It was more of, "I don't understand." But who does understand? No one can give an answer to that question; it doesn't exist to us alone. But my faith was helping me to understand and guiding me to answering that question. This was just a hurdle in my life that all 5'2(and 3/4) of me will have to jump to get to the next thing. It will make me stronger, physically and mentally. It will make me work harder. And through all of it, I need to remember that somewhere, someone has it a lot worse than I do. So, I have begun to spend more prayer time for those people, and for all of you who support me. And when it comes time to pray for my own health I've decided to keep it short and to the point. All I say to God now is, "Spirits up, faith strong, and body moving." If he helps with that, I can do the rest.

Sorry to get a little preachy on everyone today. I just write what comes to mind. If you are offended or don't like this kind of talk remember one thing: You really can't beat up a kid with cancer, can you?

I Can Be Weak.
12/22/2011

The stress was really starting to get to me. I am trying so hard to please everyone and be this pillar of strength, but I need time to be a little selfish too. I don't know the rules of cancer; as a daughter, a sister, a friend, a girlfriend; I don't understand any of it. Keeping up with this phone call, and this thank you card, and the holidays, it's just so much right now. I'd give anything to not be sick, but I am. I am sick and there will be days when I just have to be sick. Some days I need to hurt and I need to slow down, but I need everyone to be ok with it. This was hard, I knew it would be, but I don't like to be weak. And I know everyone reading this will just say, "You have to be strong." *I know*. I am strong, but I am young, and I am scared, and I need some time to be that way. I went out to dinner with friend last night; one who was a person I looked up to for a long time, and still do. She told me I need to let this happen, and I need to let myself feel bad and weak and take the time to deal with everything. She was the first person to say this. I know everyone just assumes that's something I should know, but it isn't my style. And this friend knows that. She was right. Out of all the people who have fought this battle and are fighting it, one of us should put together a cancer etiquette book. Or maybe I am the only one who is more wrapped up in pleasing everyone else than worrying about my own mental stability. My thought process is: Act fine, be fine. But what the hell is fine? So far, fine is me laughing it off and just going with the flow. So far, fine has gotten my appointments pushed back and starting chemo further away. Screw fine. I'm sick of it. So, hello world; hello everyone reading this; hello family; here I am at a weak point. This is it. I can be weak and strong at the same time. I can be weak, but still have no doubt in my mind that I am winning. I can be weak. *I can be weak.* I just needed to be a little weak right now. Besides, isn't it a sign of strength to admit to a little weakness?

Another surgery tomorrow; I'll be fine.

———

And there it was, my first breakdown of cancer. There was a song by Taylor Swift that was entitled *Eyes Open*, It perfectly described the way I was feeling through most of my battle. The lyrics are:

> "Everybody's waiting for you to breakdown
> Everybody's watching to see the fallout
> Even when you're sleeping, sleeping
> Keep your eyes open."

I felt as though I had this constant crowd of people around me just waiting for me to break. And I didn't want to. Making the phone calls to the people I cared about and telling them that I was sick was as vulnerable as I wanted to get. As much as I wanted people around, I wanted them to stop waiting for the water works and the questioning life. I just wanted to breathe without someone making sure I was doing so.

I had no idea that through this emotional blog I would gain even more support. The way I thought about things was that I needed to be this pillar of strength for everyone, I couldn't be weak because that would cause fear for others. The truth was, I needed that moment. I needed to show that I was scared in order for my family and friends to see that I needed help. After this breakdown, my family started to help me with all the thank you cards, phone calls, and taking time to just be me. I wasn't a fan of the attention and the worrying, but that's what family does in times of crisis. I realized in that moment, that I could be scared. All it took was someone giving me permission, and telling me that it's ok to be scared as long as I keep fighting.

A Little Bit Stronger
12/23/2011

Fitting that the first song I heard this morning after last night's breakdown was *A Little Bit Stronger,* by Sara Evans. I needed that though, and the responses I received were, as always, amazing.

I had surgery on my neck today, I look a little like the bride of Frankenstein, but I am so excited to be one step closer to recovery. With surgery they took half of the tumor from my neck, apparently they really had to dig and tug at it. I was out, thank goodness. I'm not even in that much pain, but when you have two knee surgeries under your belt you're kind of a pro, I guess! Saddest part of the whole day was waking up and having my knees hurt worse then my neck! What am I going to do with myself? I've been promising the boyfriend that after I beat cancer, I'll be a normal girl for a while…I hope I can deliver! I'm pretty anxious to take the bandages off tomorrow, and see what kind of scar I'll be working with. The doctors told me I'll need a good story for it; I feel like beating cancer is a good enough story for me. I should be starting chemo next week;

hopefully my holiday plans won't be ruined, but all in all I just want to be healthy again. Seems like I'll actually follow through with a New Year's resolution for once. How bout that? A silver lining!

Had some of the girls stop over tonight. Visits like that are much needed! The distraction actually helped me shake off some of the sickness from surgery. At first they were all looking at me like they had no idea what to say. I don't blame them, so obviously that's when I start throwing out the cancer jokes. At first everyone is taken aback by it, but then they see I'm ok, so it works.

I feel like I should address the breakdown a little bit. You know, at first I just wrote it in a word document and thought about saving it for myself. But my whole goal with this blog was to help myself, others, and to keep my whole support system in the know. I still have moments where I think, "Do I really want my business out there for everyone?" And it's weird, but I do. It's easy for me to do this; I have always loved helping people, and like to think that I am helping others while I help myself. The distraction is perfect, I love getting feedback from people, and I want to find ways to make this bigger and better. I think the breakdown and the blog and the responses kind of opened my eyes a little bit too. I am sick and it's just starting to sink in. I mean, yeah, I am tired all the time, I get chest pains, and there are times when my insides feel like someone lit them on fire. But none of it ever hit me like it did last night.

I realize now that it is important to be vulnerable and to cry at times. And I realize now that I have to have the bad moments to get to the good ones. Chemo is going to be the next big hurdle for me. But I promise everyone and myself, I won't let it keep me down. I'll be at the lacrosse games, even if it means coaching from the press box. I'll be in class, even if I have to ask for extra help. And all in all, I'll just be me. Spirits Up, Faith Strong, Body Moving. (Especially the knees!)

Cancer's Holiday Vacation
12/28/2011

It's been a bit since I've posted anything. Happy Holidays everyone! I am so glad I was able to enjoy Christmas with my family.

I was struggling from the neck surgery for a few days, but I'm starting to feel a lot better. Physically that is. I don't think I will get used to waiting around for results and hearing from the doctors. I completely understand that it is the holidays, don't get me wrong, everyone should be with their families this time of year, but I think we should remember that cancer doesn't take a holiday vacation. So, my results from surgery were delayed, which in turn delayed my start of chemo. And, the more time I have to sit and think about it, the more I want to just wait until after the New Year to start treatment. Of course you can imagine my parents weren't happy when I first threw the idea out there, but there isn't too much to be happy with when it comes to cancer. Every time my mom looked at my neck where the incision was her little fists ball up, and she tells me she hates cancer. I do too, Momma. So, when we started talking about me waiting another week for chemo, my parents both wanted me to start right away. But, I have New Years plans! Cancer had already taken away too much from me, I want to be able to celebrate the New Year like a normal twenty-two year old and then the next day I'll be a cancer patient again.

I woke up to a text from my mom this morning. "Call me when u r up, I want to discuss something with u." Great! You know, sometimes Moms' texting is awesome, and other times it's just another outlet to be in some kind of trouble or disappointing situation. *Don't even* get me started with mothers on Facebook! haha love you moo. Anyways, I called my mom, and thought it would be news about my results and starting my chemo this week. Instead it was about how her and dad decided I was right. They want me to have time to spend with the boyfriend and to have a last *hoorah*! before chemo. Mom even counted my antibiotics and said I'll be done in enough time to enjoy some adult beverages on New Year's Eve. Sorry Doc, looks like you'll be waiting on me this time. Sucks.

Some of you may think I'm crazy, and maybe I am. But cancer will be taking a holiday vacation, and I couldn't be more excited for it.

Bald is Beautiful. Says My Bald Brother!
01/03/2012

Happy New Year! As you all know, I decided to take a vacation from cancer and celebrate the New Year like a normal twenty-two year old. And I am glad that I did! I had an amazing five days off and now I'm ready to take this thing down.

On the first day of my *vacation,* my boyfriend and I went to my apartment; I wanted to make sure the place was still standing, and wanted to set up my new TV for whenever I am back there. On the way, my mom called and said she had heard from the doctors about my neck biopsy and chemo schedule. At first she was only going to tell me that little bit of info because I had declared a cancer holiday. But I pushed her for more and was crushed by the news. During my first meeting with my oncologist, he had told me that I would be receiving four drugs in a forty-five minute session. When they called my mom, the forty-five minutes stretched to *four hours*! Seriously? So, obviously the next thing that comes to mind is that I am going to feel terrible after that. The doctors said everyone reacts differently, but how the hell does someone sit there having chemicals pumped into their system for four hours and feel good the next day? Needless to say, I am not pleased with this news. Want the cherry on top? When we first met and he said forty-five minutes, I was also told most people don't lose their hair anymore. Now, we are being told most people do lose their hair, some people just have their hair thin out, but most *lose* it. This is not ok. You can tell me all you want about how hair is hair and health is what matters, but you tell me what twenty-two year old female wants to be bald. And maybe I won't lose it, but the fear of it is enough. I started crying immediately, and was pretty emotional the rest of the day after that news. I broke down pretty bad that night. It wasn't just the hair; it was the whole process. Dealing with the four hour treatments and the fact that I have cancer hit me. I was trying to move forward and just got blindside tackled by James Harrison. The next day I even cried straightening my hair! Does cancer make someone more emotional?

The rest of my cancer vacation was amazing though. I hardly ever stopped moving and had a great time with my boyfriend and his family. I think things like that will help me get through this nonsense. I am going to keep giving myself breaks and things to look forward to. And I decided, when I beat it, I am going to Harry Potter World! I've never been to Universal Studios or Disney World, so I figured they'd be the perfect celebration.

As for the fears ahead, I'm ready to face them. Tomorrow starts treatment and I plan on having my laptop with me to write out what I am feeling. And if I lose my hair, I know I won't handle it well, but I'll manage. Can you believe when I was little I used to beg to shave my head? I hated my hair! I used to cut all my Barbie's hair and got into so much trouble for it. Is this karma? I swear, Barbie never complained about her new look! If it comes down to it though, I won't complain much either. I will do what I have to do to be strong again and get my life where I want it to be. I already have one scar from cancer that I am wearing proud; at least being bald is temporary.

I'm strong enough to do all of this, I have the biggest team behind me, and I am ready to win.

One step closer...
01/04/2012

I'm trying to go to bed right now but I am currently being reminded of the battle that was being fought inside my body. Today was chemo day; it was crazy. But for the record; I've got this.

My morning started with a visit to the neck surgeon at 8:30; she said my incision looks fine; it split open in two spots, but since I admitted it to my parents, I might as well tell all of you that I ended up peeling the glue off! *Oops!* I'm not good with bandages and stuff like that. Oh well, it will heal! After that, we went to see my oncologist, discussed my treatment plan and all the possible outcomes. The first time we saw him, he said no radiation because it can lead to heart failure and future cancers and now all the sudden he's saying it's a possibility. I've already made my decision that I will do extra chemo to avoid that risk. After we met with him, we went on to my first chemo appointment. It started late so I was pretty antsy and when they wanted to start, all my veins decided to hide, so that was awesome! A pharmacist came in to explain the side affects of all my drugs. My treatment was ABVD, that's four different drugs that can all cause some of the following: nausea, hair loss, fevers, chills, a whole bunch of bowel issues, rashes, mouth sores, and a whole bunch of others I just decided to ignore. Pretty much chemo sucks but will make me healthy. Bring it on cancer! Finally, I was able to start my treatment; the nurse administered the first two drugs directly into my IV, they took about ten minutes. The third was a drip that took ten minutes and the final one was a two-hour drip. It had to be given with other fluids because there is a possibility that it will burn when going into my vein. The other thing I learned today is that I pretty much have to tell my doctors and nurses every little detail from now on. I'm so terrible at that. This blog should help though; I can just read to them what I was feeling on a certain date. Current update: nauseous, tired, and a whole lot of chest pain keeping me up. Oh, I forgot to mention the pharmacist said I should be noticing the lump on my neck shrink fairly quickly. Also, the biggest lymph node in my chest measures at 8 cm and that will start shrinking as well. I was also told I'll start noticing hair loss within two weeks. They said it wouldn't come out in patches it will just thin. I can handle whatever cancer throws at me though. I also had a social worker stop by today. It was funny because she asked if I have told people what is going on and I'm pretty sure I caught her off guard when I told her I made a website about it!

And for all you movie buffs out there I'll tell ya this: Chemo is highly fabricated in the movies! I wasn't puking my life up in a bucket, and I actually had a private room. It was little but I liked it better then being in the open rooms you see on TV sometimes. My nurse was great. She actually just battled breast cancer this past summer. We will see what tomorrow brings in how I react to treatment, but so far so good!

Did I mention my parents might get me a puppy for a chemo present! Dad said no at first but was Googling them at treatment. He just can't say no to the Daisy/Bri combo! Haha love ya, pop!

Check back later, I'm sure I'll update you on how the day after treatment feels!…Spirits up, faith strong, body moving.

―――

While it was partially true that chemo is pretty fabricated in movies, not everyone had the same side effects. Some people do throw up, and there are open rooms, but patients with shorter treatment times typically use those. One of the worst parts of chemo were the tastes, the memory of smells, and the fact that once you eat something at chemo, it will be awhile before you eat it again. I still have moments when I smell chemo. It wasn't the actual drugs that you smell, it was memories like hospital hand soap, or in my case the bath and body antibacterial I always used. I would get nauseous just thinking about these things. I heard someone explain chemo as pumping gasoline into your body and then lighting your insides on fire. That was the most spot on description I can give you all. It was horrible and I wouldn't wish it upon my worst enemy. I always find it crazy that something that will save your life had to first make you feel like your life is ending.

There were a few tricks I learned throughout my treatments, the first one I highly recommend is chewing gum when they are flushing your port or IVs with saline. At first the saline taste won't bother you, but after two or three rounds of chemo it will start to make you sick. Simply because of the anticipation of what was to come. Chewing gum during this masks the taste of the saline. My parents and I often discovered that if I ate, I was less nauseous. I would eat through chemo and it seemed as though I wouldn't become too sick. There were plenty of times when I did not want to eat, but I knew it was best. I still had to take plenty of nausea medicine, but this little food trick, that was told to me by one of my nurses helped immensely.

Nausea, Chest Pains, and Mouth Sores. Oh My!
01/07/2012

I told you all to check back soon and I let ya down! My bad, I have cancer ;). Well, let's see what you've missed. Sleep, nausea, sleep, sleep, visitors, sleep. Oh and the mouth sores are starting! Yipee.

The past couple of days have been a mix of emotions for me. One minute I am so excited because chemo wasn't crushing me, and the next minute I am so scared that this is a one-time pain free-chemo pass. I hate everything about this disease. I hate the pains, I hate the way it makes my family feel, I hate sitting in a cancer chair for four hours with chemicals being pumped in to me. And guess what? I've only had one treatment! I'll get through it, but I obviously don't have to like it.

We did some traveling today to celebrate my niece's second birthday. While I enjoyed every minute of hanging out with that little goof, it took a lot out of me. As I was attempting to sleep in the car I could over hear some of my parents conversations about me being sick. And while I'd rather know what they are feeling then have them hide it, I get so angry at everything. Why did I have to get this nasty disease? As I was lying there listening to them talk about it I decided I couldn't be happier that it's happening to me. I would be a mess if one of my parents were going through this. I am strong and young, as much as everyone can say "You never want to see your child go through this," I'll show you a child who thanks God that it isn't their mom or dad. I couldn't agree with my mom more though, when I hear her say that she hates this dumb cancer and just wishes she could rip it out of me.

Last night, sleeping was a challenge. My chest was killing me and my mouth started causing an issue. My mouth feels like there are pins in it and my tongue is so itchy! Only explanation: mouth sores. Gross. Cancer sure does know how to make a girl feel pretty! For those of you who haven't seen me in awhile, you should know that I decided to get braces at the end of October. Yeah, 22, braces, I know. My thought process was that my smile was the one thing I was really self-conscious about. I wasn't going to need to wear a mouth guard this year, so why not take care of my teeth? Well, now with day one of mouth sores, I'm contemplating getting my dad's pliers and getting rid of the braces! Hello salt water gargling! You are about to be my new best friend! Honestly though, besides the chest pains, how can I complain when it could be a hundred times worse.

That's where my head is at today. Yeah, I have cancer, but it's curable. I have mouth sores, gross, but they'll go away. And I have extreme chest pains, but that just means the medicine is doing its job. Somewhere in this world someone is fighting challenges much worse than what I am facing. Even close friends of mine are dealing with situations that are just as hard, if not harder than what I am going through. So, next time you want to complain because you are having a bad day, think about the people who are legitimately having the worst days of their lives. Don't you feel a little bit more grateful for the cards you've been dealt? If the answer is no, I am sorry to hear that, just know that as you support me, I also support *you*. Keep your head up and stand proud. I'm doing it everyday.

One Day at a Time
01/10/2012

Yesterday was bad. Today, so far so good! I woke up yesterday and felt incredible; I thought I could run a marathon. But as I thought about what to do with my energy, my mind just kept drifting to a bad place. All I could think was, "Yeah, I feel great today but in nine more days, I get four more hours of chemicals, and goodbye energy!" Then I would think about how this is a roller coaster; I will be on for the next four to six months! Mentally that is exhausting. Think about it; one day you feel on top of the world, like nothing can go wrong, but you actually know that soon comes pain. How terrible is that! It's safe to say that yesterday I lost sight of living day by day.

Like I said, when I woke up I felt incredible, then around 6 o'clock I had the worst chest pains that I have ever had. I didn't know what to do or why I was having them. My mom called the clinic and I had to talk to the doctor that was on call. He told me to go to the emergency room to get checked out and that if I couldn't get there fast enough I should call an ambulance. Now, I know that sounds pretty scary, but I didn't want to do it. I wanted to see if the pain would get worse or go away. My parents were waiting for my word and I just felt that if it were emergency status, I'd be bawling my eyes out. Curse my high pain tolerance! I don't know when to complain and when not to; is that weird? I don't know what pain is too much and I don't want to go in for a hangnail. These bills add up! So, I didn't go and luckily within a couple of hours the pain started to subside. I am not good at this being sick thing, when my mom handed me the phone to talk to the doctor she had to say, "*Don't lie!*" I've never admitted the pain I am in. Ask my Athletic Trainer at Slippery Rock, bless her soul, she dealt with me for four years and two knee surgeries!

Today, I woke up with little pain and much better spirits. I'm actually about to go out to lunch with a friend in a bit and I am so pumped to be out of the house! And in regards to all the response I got from the last blog, I got the magic mouthwash! It's absolutely disgusting, but incredible! Before I got it though, I stuck to the salt-water gargle. I was headed to the kitchen to gargle and asked my dad if he wanted to have a gargle party with me. He came out to the kitchen and I'd take a sip to gargle with and we'd both start dancing like idiots. It was so ridiculous and I don't know if anyone has seen my dad's moves but I ended up spitting salt water everywhere! With all the noise and laughter we were making we decided to invite mom. Please picture me with a mouthful of salt water and my parents dancing like fools. It was one of the best moments of cancer yet! Mom claims to be Puerto Rican, but not with those moves, lady!

Oh, and I also had to hear all about how they had to clean salt water off every window and cupboard in the kitchen!

Anyways, I have to get ready for lunch. Remember: Just live life one day at a time, no sense in worrying about what hasn't happened yet.

———

Seeing as how I had cancer, I think it is socially acceptable to explain how the chest pains that night miraculously subsided! Of course in movies you see cancer patients using medical marijuana all the time. It always seems to make them feel better and help them to make it through. I had multiple people of all ages telling me I should invest in some marijuana to help me with nausea and pain. So, I did! My parents weren't fond of the idea, but if it helped me they were all for it. So, with these chest pains I decided to try it. My grandparents were staying at our house at this point and my grandma knew the amount of pain I was in. I didn't have the heart to let them know I was going to the basement to toke it up! I remember coming back upstairs as the pain was subsiding and asking grandma for a delicious piece of her freshly made apple pie! Then she said, "It's crazy how that pain has just gone away!" Now, to this day, I am not sure if my grandparents realize what I did, it was never really a discussion between us. But I found something that eased the pain, and I will recommend it to any cancer patient. Any form of relief you can find in such horrible pain is well worth it.

Nothing Profound, Just Procrastination
01/12/2012

I'm procrastinating right now. I need to be packing for Philadelphia this weekend, but instead I'm on here! Typical. I'm pretty sure it's mentioned somewhere on the site, but I am the Grad Assistant for my lax team at Slippery Rock this year. Tomorrow, Lindsay (the assistant coach who yelled at me for my lump months ago) and I will be off to the Lacrosse Convention. I'm pretty excited to be getting away, but my mother had to call Linds tonight and tell her the babysitting details. I will have a special bag just for medications, hand sanitizers, and my thermometer, of course!

I start school soon, I am pretty anxious about it. It will be interesting to see how I do with school and chemo. My professors were all ridiculously understanding during the last couple weeks of the semester, so I am not worried about how things will go from that aspect. I am more concerned about falling behind. Before my diagnosis I suffered from dizzy spells pretty frequently; it turns out, it was just the location of the lymph node in my neck causing them. But it certainly made doing homework a challenge. I couldn't focus on writing a paper because I would get into the paper and a dizzy spell would hit and I'd just lose it all. I am nervous that if chemo starts hitting me hard, school will be even more difficult. And the simple solution when times get hard would be to take time off, but I am certainly not trying to be a student forever! I mean, I hear the real world is a scary place, but I have cancer and that's scary, so bring on the real world! I was planning on finishing grad school this summer. I was going to take some extra hours and do some online courses while using my summer camp as an internship. But it looks like I won't be able to finish as quickly as I was hoping. Don't worry, I am still going to camp though. And I'll be on spring training with my team! I'll fight a doctor if I have to!

You know, some nights I lay in bed and think, *What if tomorrow I wake up and this was all some crazy, stupid, dream?* Then tomorrow comes and I am still here waiting for the next needle. On our first appointment to the oncologist my mom and I were walking through the Cleveland Clinic saying, "What if it isn't cancer?" And after awhile, dad just said, "That'd be great, but it is." Dad is good at that. He let's us play the what if game for a little bit, but right before we get too crazy with it, he brings us back down to reality. I think I'll need that in a couple of weeks. I am going to want to push through everything so I can coach, get through school, and try to be normal. But I am going to need reality checks every now and then. I don't know what future treatments have in store for me, I don't know if I will be bald, and I don't know if I will be able to finish my semester. But I do know that if treatments are bad, I will survive. If I am bald, the people who matter will not even notice. And if I can't finish my semester, I'll bust my butt to get back on track and start my life. That's all I really want after all. I just want to start my life.

I guess I'll pack now.

What a Trip!
01/14/2012

Where do I even begin? Well, I'm not in Philadelphia. Actually I didn't even make it to Slippery Rock! *Fail!* I think everyone is aware that I was in the hospital yesterday, but there's a slight chance it was an animal hospital because everyone there was slightly confused! Here's what happened.

I started my morning early, traveling through the snow to get to Lindsay's so we could make the trip to Philadelphia for the Lacrosse Convention. I ate a bowl of cereal, got in the shower, and took off. When I got to Lindsay's we hung out for a little bit and then decided to start our adventure and boy, was it an adventure! The roads were pretty messy, but that wasn't where my head was. My head was pretty much focused on my heartbeat. It was all I could hear, and it was fast. I was trying to take deep breaths and calm myself down but it wasn't working. So, I told Lindsay that something wasn't right. At that point, you could visibly see my heart beat and I made her feel it. She said, "We are close to the hospital, let's go." This time, I agreed. Have you ever been electrocuted? That tingling feeling zaps your whole body? That's what I felt. My heart felt like it was in a fistfight with my ribs and every time it hit, it would shoot tingles through my entire body. I couldn't focus on anything and I couldn't calm it down. It was the scariest and worst thing I have ever had happen to me. I legitimately thought I was having a heart attack. So we went to Grove City Hospital. Definitely not the ideal choices in hospitals, but the roads were bad and we were close.

Here is where all the fun begins! When I go to the ER I am instructed to say, "My name is Brianne Dishong, I am currently undergoing chemo therapy, and I am having chest pains." That gets me ahead of the person coughing up a lung because they chain smoke… So, they took me to a room right away. Then everything seemed to slow down. The nurse was a male, who was much more concerned with being considered the funny guy than being good at his job. And the Doctor was a nice, but overweight, smelly guy (no lie, ask Lindsay), who at one point in college wouldn't give my roommate pain killers even though her face was swollen twice the size it normally is, because he thought we were just looking to score some drugs. Anyways, he listens to my heart and tells me it sounds fine. They had a student nurse in the room that hooked me up to a heart monitor, admittedly telling me she had no idea which wires went where. Then the fun part came.

When you're dehydrated, it is much harder to find your vein. And when you're being poked more than a pincushion, you can tell when they have done it right. So the male nurse was trying to get me an IV so I could start on fluids. He puts the needle in my arm and just kind of fishes around for a vein. It isn't comfortable, but I am pretty good with pain so it was never an issue for me. He said he thought he had a vein but it wasn't drawing blood, doesn't make sense does it? Then he tried to flush the IV. Now, being that I now frequently have needles in my arm I have gotten used to tasting the saline when they flush the IV. And I told him exactly that. He said not every patient had that sensation and that the drip was flowing nicely, and to let him know if it hurt. So, I proceeded to tell him that I have tasted the saline *everytime* and that the IV was hurting. *I don't complain, ever.* But he said, "Well it's working, so you'll get used to it." I proceeded to tell him something wasn't right and then my bicep started hurting. Now, I like to joke about how ripped I am, but we all know that's a lie. My bicep looked like it was huge... not normal. And this man told me that it was just as hard as my forearm so there's nothing wrong with the IV. I have lived with my arms for 22 years. I know when I flex that my forearm and bicep may feel as hard as each other, but with lack of exercise and sports in my life it is not that hard anymore. So, I am in so much pain and screaming at this man to get the IV out. My skin feels as if it is about to split open and my bicep is just growing. Finally another nurse heard me and came in the room and said, "That is infiltrated, get it out of her!" Thank

God she said that because I was about to make a mess and rip the damn thing out myself. Finally, relief! The IV was out but my arm was throbbing, that nurse just kind of quietly disappeared, coming back every now and then, only to have Lindsay and I ignore his bad jokes. I think he got the hint when he called himself fat and we didn't respond.

You think that's good? It gets better! So after all of that, I still haven't gotten any fluids. They send in another nurse and a blood work guy to try to draw blood and start my IV. So, the blood work guy was doing his thing on my arm that was just inflated like a bad balloon animal, and he just keeps saying, "Man it's hot in here, is it hot in here?" Oh, forgot to mention he is a heavyset dude too. I look at the man and there was sweat pouring off his head, my thought: "Oh, this is sanitary." He keeps struggling for a bit, and then announces he needs to go wipe off his head. Yup, *wipe off his head*. So, he comes back in and starts squeezing my arm like it's the last bit of toothpaste and he really needs to get it out, painful, but gets blood this way. As he is doing that another nurse was on my left arm poking around to start an IV. I mention that she should try my hand and she does, she finds a vein and flushes and I say, "Oh, saline, yeah I told you I'd taste it!" Finally, my IV is started. Meanwhile sweatbox had left the room. Lindsay had been in and out on phone calls with my mom and she doesn't handle the needles well, so I am sure this wasn't fun for her. She comes back in the room and says, "What did you do to

Shane? (sweatbox)" I ask her what she is talking about and she informs me that he is on a stretcher with his shirt off being admitted into the E.R. He left my room and passed out! Seriously? Where the hell am I? The kicker was, I was just telling Lindsay how interesting it was that I am being taken care of by all these people who look so unhealthy they could just keel over at any minute. I have never had a point proven so quickly and so extreme!

I could keep complaining about the hospital, but I won't. The good news was my tests came back fine, they pumped me with two bags of fluid and let me go. I just need to be sure not to get dehydrated anymore. Today, I am bruised on both arms, and can barely straighten the right one without pain. But I survived. And throughout the hell of that place, I managed to keep smiling, keep cracking jokes, and the doctor told me it was an honor to meet someone with my spirit in this situation and that I was an inspiration. Thanks dude. Means a lot, but can I have ice for my arm or something? I'm kidding, I appreciated him saying that but I wanted out of there.

I stayed with Lindsay and Mike, had fun, and my mom now had proof that I have excellent babysitters for when I am back at school! I'm so grateful to have Lindsay and that she stuck by my side through that and all that will come. What a trip! I like to think of it as proof that my spirits are up, my faith is strong, and my body is moving!

I need to go chug some Gatorade now.

There was a moment in the hospital when I began to cry, Lindsay asked me if I was in pain and my response was, "No, I was just adding up the bills in my head!" Maybe this sounds crazy, who can put a price on their life? But I didn't think of it in this way. All I could think about was how I am a college student, who shouldn't be living off of her parents anymore, and all I keep doing is spending their money. Now my parents told me a million times that I don't need to worry about that because I am worth every penny. But it's just the principle of it. I hated thinking about the money being spent, but in the end it was a dumb thing to worry about. Sometimes it was hard to remember that *life-threatening disease* is exactly how it sounds. And to survive it, means getting the care you need when you need it.

The Sixth-Grade Boy Who Changed My Life
01/17/2012

Every night, right when I lay down to go to sleep, the worry sets in. It's like as soon as I hit my pillow, no matter how exhausted I am fear and anxiety overcome me. Even on the good days this happens. Thousands of questions consume me; will I be sick tomorrow? will I lose my hair? Will chemo eventually knock me down? Will the next few months go quickly? On and on. Sometimes it brings me down, and although that is perfectly fine, every now and then I need a way to ease my mind. I have been trying to figure it out for a while now. Some nights I will lay flat on my back and start at my toes and think, "Ok, relax the toes, now the ankles, the calves, the knees, etc." That barely works. Sometimes I try counting, that never works. And sometimes I just let the thoughts come, until eventually I am way too exhausted to think about it anymore. Last night was different.

I went to lunch with my uncle yesterday. It was a lot of fun to spend time with him and just talk about things to someone who doesn't see it everyday. When we were talking, I expressed my fear for future chemo treatments.

And Uncle Matt just said, "You have to treat it like you did a Lacrosse game." He said it so simply and it made more sense to me than anything. I have to treat this as another opponent. Each treatment is just another game. I know the scouting report, Drug #1: Fast, can catch you off guard if you're sleeping, with all intentions to knock you off your feet. Drug #2: Also fast, you have to be quick to react, don't let it catch you off guard. Drug #3: Strong. Drug #4: Can burn you, keep your feet moving and your mind right. So, being that defense is all I've ever known, I've got this…I let the drugs burn me once and go to goal and I ended up in the ER, but I never let anything take me twice. Besides, with my team, no one stands a chance.

As I was thinking about this last night, I was reminded of all my athletic rituals. The thing that really made me open my eyes was remembering a picture that hung in my locker at Slippery Rock throughout all four years of my career there. I don't know how I could've ever forgotten this story, but it came to me at a time when I needed it the most. In sixth grade, I met a boy who was obnoxious, rude, a self-proclaimed ladies man, funny, determined, and everyone loved him. His name was Shane Cook; he had muscular dystrophy. He had the smallest body, a high-pitched voice, a big head, and a vocabulary that was not parent-approved. He was the kid who during those embarrassing movies about sex would look at you, blow kisses, and just make you want to smack him. Well, in sixth grade, the entire grade goes to a sleep-away camp; our class went to Pilgrim Hills. At Pilgrim Hills, they had a team challenge adventure course; the only challenge I remember is the tire wall. It probably wasn't as tall as I picture it to be now, but the challenge was that your whole team had to get to the other side, but only one person could go through each tire. Shane was a member of my team and of course he wanted to climb to the top. The teachers, the adventure people, and the parent chaperones were all huddled up discussing if Shane could go to the top or if it would be safer for him to climb through the bottom tire. Shane didn't care for the conversation at all, he walked right passed their huddle and started climbing. They didn't notice until he was nearing the top and turned around and gave them all the finger. It was the most amazing thing I have seen to this day. That was the kind of kid Shane was, he could not be told *no*. He let you know exactly what was on his mind and he was fearless. Shane passed away that summer, he was the first friend I had ever had to say goodbye to. I found out at a summer basketball game, and from that day forward, no matter what sport I played, I wore the initials *SRC* on my shoe. Before every game, I'd look at his initials and remind myself that I play for those who can't. The picture of Shane climbing that tire wall hung in my locker at Slippery Rock. In the picture, there were hands of someone trying to help him just out of reach. He never wanted the help; he never really needed it; he knew he was strong enough to do it.

And now ten years later, he still reminds me that I am strong enough too. He's my inspiration, he always had been. And that picture is something I will cherish for the rest of my life. How crazy is it that back then, I was probably taking the picture to be a rebel, cracking up at the fact that Shane just flicked off everyone we were supposed to be completely respectful to? And now it's something that I have used to keep me focused and going for what I want, not letting anyone tell me *no*.

I am a true believer that everyone comes into your life for a reason. I used to think Shane was my inspiration to keep fighting everyone telling me I was too small to play a sport. But he was in my life for much more than that. He was in my life to show me that not one person, or one obstacle, can tell you *no*, unless you let it.

Finding memories like those of Shane's courage and defiance saved me at this point in treatments. Things were hitting me hard and I was becoming scared. I didn't let anyone see it, but the fear was there. To this day when I look at that picture I can remember Shane's voice. It makes me smile every time.

At the beginning of my diagnosis, my mom's best friend asked if she could hold a benefit for me to help with the expenses of chemo and even help purchase a wig. At first we were weary of it, we didn't expect many people to come and didn't want to seem like we were asking for money. My family is very low-key, after I graduated high school, half of the town thought that my parents had moved! Being in the spotlight was something we were not at all used to, but the outcome was incredible.

If Seeing is Believing…
01/22/2012

A lot has happened since my last blog, but how do you follow up a blog like that one?

First, let me thank everyone and anyone who was a part of the spaghetti dinner this Friday night. It's one thing to see the hits my blog gets, but it was like a different world witnessing that event. If I didn't believe all the support I had before, I was definitely seeing it. It was great seeing all of you and feeling the support of my team. And for those of you who didn't make it, I know you are here too, don't worry! Also, if I missed anyone when I had to take off, I apologize.

I was a little anxious on Friday with the event and didn't sleep much the night before. So, throughout the evening I started to feel pretty sick and had to escape twice. I didn't sleep much Friday night either, so yesterday was quite a mess for me. A lot of random tears! Sometimes when I start to feel really bad, all I can do is cry. That may seem weird, but it's all I can do. The combination of fear, pain, fatigue, and just overall feeling like crap, just gets the best of me.

It's so weird really, I wish I could explain it better. I hit this wall, where everything hurts, everything aches, I just want to sleep but even that is uncomfortable. It isn't like I am in crazy pain, I just get so weak and uncomfortable at times. It's all a part of cancer, I guess.

I also had a personal event occur that I had been dreading happen while getting ready for Friday night. As I was folding a bunch of trifolds for dinner that had all the information about the event; my medical timeline, and my future treatment dates; my hands kept getting really cold, which was common when undergoing chemotherapy. So, I decided I would stop doing that and start straightening my hair. Now, everyone is used to losing a little hair everyday while they're getting ready, but I was *not* losing a little hair. I was literally pulling out clumps. Not like the clumps you see on TV or in movies, it doesn't happen like that. It is more of a thinning process, and thank God I have a lot of hair or I would've been bald at the benefit. So, I called my mom, crying my eyes out obviously, and she started crying saying she was leaving work now and don't worry she'd be home soon. Which I am glad, but she couldn't put my hair back in my head. Then I get a call from my dad, who was also crying. Do you know how hard it is to hear your dad cry? I mean moms are one thing, but dad? It's like a knife to the heart. But he was on his way home too. I just kept straightening my hair waiting for my mom to come in and see the pile lying in front of me. When she came in, I was feeling a little better but still crying. It's hard to be twenty-two and watching your hair fall out. It is like a realization that this beast inside me does exist. Next we went to the hall where the benefit was being held to see the volunteers and thank them for their time. One of my very good friends who is a hair stylist was there and when I saw her I almost immediately started crying. Luckily, she is the type of friend who, when we are together, we spend most of the time laughing at our (or mostly her) expense! Anyways, I showed her the picture of how much hair I had just lost, and she simply said it's time to move to the next step. So next Saturday; my mom, my friend, and I will be wig shopping! I have decided today that when it starts to get really bad, I will be shaving it myself. Call it a control thing, but if this is going to happen it's going to be on my terms.

I'd really like to take the time to extend my appreciation again to everyone who was involved in the benefit. And to everyone who had just been apart of my support team in general. I have been so blessed to have parents who have done so much for me, and for our community with sports, and to see everyone coming to our aide, who we haven't seen in years, meant more to me than any of you could ever know. My family and I have recently become aware of a mother of three who was diagnosed with cancer, and we have decided to start paying it forward now. I know a lot of you were curious about the, *Fight like a Girl* shirts and if you could buy them or not. Well, we are going to get more printed and I will be selling them from this site. All the proceeds will be going to this woman and her family.

Fighters need to fight, and winners will win together.

Still I Rise, Still I Fight
01/24/2012

Today was a great day. I have only had a little bit of chest pain, I switched to online schooling, and I even got out of the house for a bit. Thursday, I will be going to the clinic for a newly scheduled visit. They want to hydrate me and want to discuss a few things. There was some concern with some of the symptoms I have been having. The most uncomfortable one, which was new, was that my jaw had been locking. This started the night of the spaghetti dinner, and it was so uncomfortable! I also had a rough night of trying to sleep a couple of days ago; my joints were killing me! I am used to my knees hurting and all, but this was excruciating. I ended up coming downstairs and waking my parents up because I couldn't even think straight. So, after calling the clinic we have scheduled a visit for Thursday. There was also a concern with one of my drugs, which hopefully doesn't screw anything up too bad.

My head has been in a really good place lately too. I experience some anxiety every now and then, but nothing too bad. Although, I did catch myself talking to myself today, that is not ok! I am really bummed; I can't go back to Slippery Rock. I had to drop my classes and schedule online courses, which I am so happy that I was able to do, but I miss it. And mostly, I miss my team. They have helped me through some of the most painful times of my life and it doesn't feel right not being near them. Every game I ended up standing by one of my best friends after the announcements, during the national anthem and I would say, *Still I rise*, and she would respond, "Still I fight." It was a rap song by Nicki Minaj and I was obsessed with it. Morgan preferred getting pumped up to *Space Jam*, but this was our little ritual together. She texted me tonight about reading one of my blogs and seemed a little panicked. Then, she mentioned that as she read it, *Still I rise, still I fight*, was playing in her head. It is so crazy how all these memories keep popping up in my head. It's enough to make me really wonder if those things happened just so I could get to this place. It's this place where I am seeing massive amounts of hair fall out daily, and cracking jokes about it. Where I have these hot flashes and laugh about early menopause. Where I can be a rock for my parents and make my mom scream, "*F—— cancer*," at the top of her lungs today, multiple times, to try to make her feel a little bit better. Life is crazy like that, I guess. Things that were once dumb pregame rituals can turn into something like a theme song to your life. Man, I miss my team.

I'll visit eventually, as soon as my counts are up. Until then, I guess I'll keep spending my days talking to myself and going to school online. But just like any other day, *Still I rise, Still I fight.*

———

Shortly after the benefit all the visits started to slow down. At one point I was overwhelmed by the amount of people stopping by and then it just sort of stopped. Those were the times when it was hard. I had nothing to do but to think about what was going on in my life. It was a mind game. One of the biggest mistakes I made throughout my battle was not telling people what I needed. I could've had people with me all the time; all I had to do was ask. But I was scared. I didn't want to be a needy person just because I was sick. Now, I realize it wasn't that I was needy, and none of my friends would've seen it that way, I just needed company to distract me.

This was Supposed to be My Week Away
01/26/2012

Today was a Cleveland Clinic day. It wasn't at all what I expected, but it wasn't bad. I knew the plan was to hydrate me and discuss some of the symptoms I have been having. But when we walked into the clinic, I was just angry. We had to go to the treatment room, which I wasn't expecting for some reason. As we were in the waiting room my anxiety started kicking in. I started crying for no reason at all, I hate that place, I hate everything about it. Then we went back into my chemo room, which just made me even more angry because this is supposed to be my week away from that place. Everything today set me off; the waiting room, the chemo room, the needle (and of course they didn't get me on the first try), and the two hours of fluids. I am sick of it. I am sick of being a pincushion; I am sick of hurting; I am sick of the roller coaster of health. Today was a day when I literally just wanted to say, *no*. I wished more then anything I could just stand up and say, "Nope, not me, not today. I don't want to do it, I am done." It's so hard. Obviously, I'd never throw in the towel, because that would essentially be throwing in the towel of my life. I won't have that, I have way too much to do, and a lot of proving to my parents and family that I can be normal someday! Today was just not my day.

I want a port. I am so tired of being poked, and it never works on the first try anymore. I have scars from needles in my arm. I am not ok with that. Of course I am the only one who will notice them, but it doesn't matter. I am so tired of being sick; I just want it to be over. Can I fast-forward my life for a little bit? I am done with one cycle. Which is awesome, it's one to put behind me and be done with. But a week from today, I have another treatment and I don't want the side effects that come with it. This is hard. Doctors make it sound so easy, "We will have this many cycles, and at this point it will be half-way gone, then at this time you'll be cured." No offense to anyone, but before you describe to a cancer patient what they are going to deal with, take a quick hit of those drugs yourself. *It sucks*! It sucks. Someone somewhere has it worse than I do. To that person, I sincerely apologize. I am crying over being hydrated and having a *curable* cancer. I should be slapped.

It's necessary to have these breakdowns, but now treatment is something I fear. Something that will make me better hurts me so bad. It's not fair. This thing isn't fair. But nothing is fair, and someone, somewhere, has it worse than I do. I'll get over this breakdown and be ready for more. But don't let anyone convince you beating cancer is easy. I don't care what stage it was or what kind. But today's lesson for myself was just to keep pushing. Keep fighting. There's nothing else to do. I was handed a crappy situation, but it's because I am strong enough. I am strong enough to take this on and come out on the other side cured and ready to live my life. And I can promise you when I am done; I *will* live my life. Today I do need a little help with the spirits being up, the faith being stronger, and the body moving a little bit better.

A Weekend to Remember
01/28/2012

What a weekend! After my breakdown the other day, I was still pretty emotional. I had planned to get a haircut on Friday and was just considering getting a trim. When I woke up Friday morning my hair was a tangled mess, and I was forced to brush it. That's how it happens by the way, it isn't just like my hair falls out nicely, it is a complete mess. When I wake up there's hair on my pillow and always a huge knot on my head. It doesn't matter if I wear my hair up or down when I sleep; it always turns into a nest, big enough to house an entire family of birds. When I brush through it, I can't feel anything, no pulling, no pain. All that happens is tons of hair filling the brush or falling into my lap. Friday was extremely bad, so I decided enough was enough and I wanted it chopped. Remember how I discussed my beautiful long hair don't care? Well it's gone. I worked so hard on getting that hair to grow and be exactly how I wanted it and now… Well at least I still have hair for now, right? So, my mom took the afternoon off to go get my haircut by my friend, Amy (she does a great job you should def use her!). When I walked into Amy's salon, I immediately started crying. I was still emotional from the breakdown, plus I *loved* my hair! But after a minute or two of tears I just said, "Ok, cut it off and do what you want." I haven't had my hair this short since fourth grade! But I like it a lot. I now know that when it is growing back and reaches this length I'll be happy.

I am still not 100 percent sure I will completely lose my hair, but at the rate it's falling out I am preparing myself for *no hair days*. Today, my mom, Amy, and myself went wig shopping. I don't know if you know this about me but hair creeps me out. If it's not mine, I don't want to touch it. I even get creeped out watching the movie Tangled! So, we pull up to the wig place, and immediately I am grossed out. Right in the window was a head with ridiculous makeup and a wig on. Not ok. Why can't it just be like a wig stand? Or just a head with no facial features? Then we go in to the store. *Oh my goodness*! There were way too many heads staring at me in there. To say it was overwhelming is an understatement. I mean, I guess I don't think about wig shops often, but take a time out and picture one if you haven't been. If you can't picture it, I will literally send you pictures because we took some! So, we meet this woman, who actually never even gave us her name. And she just keeps talking about wigs and referring to the wigs as, "She," and, "her." Seriously lady? *It's fake hair; stop*! We all tell her that I want something straight, simple, and close to my color, I want it to be as natural as possible. "Well, we just got her in, I *love* her, you should try her on," says Wig Woman. All right, lady let's get on with it. She sits me in a little booth and sets up a chair for my mom and Amy. We were all glancing at each other every now and then with weary expressions. I start trying on the wigs with this woman's help. The poor lady didn't know how to handle my widow's peak, as it kept showing under the wigs. I just told her it's fine, I've accepted my widow's *body*, as I call it, and Amy asked her if she thought it would grow back in. I kept telling Wig Woman I did not want bangs and boy was I right! I *cannot* pull off bangs. Finally, I try on her "girl," the one she just "loves," and I am not sure if she means *love* like, "I *love* cake." I think it was more than that. But anyways, I really liked it. It was a little lighter color than my hair and had some highlights in it. But I might as well change things up a bit! The only issue was that the wig wasn't cooperating with my side part. As she was trying (and failing) to convince us that the wig would 'train,' Amy was getting a little feisty. It's a synthetic wig, so it won't train like human hair. Amy was trying to ask her if she was sure it would train, because I was about to spend a lot of money on this thing! Wig Woman was not answering the question, she kept saying to Amy, "Well look at your hair, What if I messed your hair up?" *not* appreciated. Then WW asks if I have a beautician, when I pointed to Amy, I think it *alllllll* made sense to her. Poor Lady. She finally answered Amy's questions and we bought the wig. Seeing as how she referred to the wig like it was alive, we decided I needed to name it. I am now the proud owner of Lola! She is sitting in another room in the house, (because it freaks me out to look at it), with a clip in, being "trained." I am happy with the purchase and it was a pretty funny experience too.

Tonight, the high school girl's basketball teams held games as fundraisers for me. Growing up, basketball was my life; a gym had always been home to me. But walking into that gym tonight meant more to me then ever before, just in a different way. It wasn't the same feeling I had during our State pep rally in that gym, and it certainly wasn't the feeling of eighty suicides after a bad game or day of terrible free throws. It was humbling, heartwarming, and inspiring. The girls all played in lime green socks with lime green ribbons. They warmed up in, "Fight like a girl" shirts that a lot of the fans were sporting as well. They showed me that once you are a Bulldog, you are always a Bulldog. It was weird to be back there seeing these girls, who used to be these cute little things running around basketball camp, supporting my fight in cancer. It was truly incredible. I had younger girls, who were all in their travel basketball shorts and their lime green shirts asking me for my autograph, like I was some kind of celebrity. One thing that was extremely incredible to me was the Hudson team. Their coach, who I played against for many years, came right over to talk to my family. And their starters would be announced and then come shake my hand. Even my boyfriend's high school boys lacrosse team in Erie, Pa, played in a tournament with green socks and the number 4 on their chin straps today! I've never even met these boys! It's just crazy.

I know I have a big support system, but you all make me feel like I can take on the world. And for that I am sincerely blessed. So, bring on the bad days. I can take them. Because memories like the ones from this weekend will get me through anything. And whenever you are feeling down, remember that even when you feel alone, there is always someone who will have your back. And if you don't believe it, give me a call. I'll fight for you and I'll fight with you.

―――

Growing up in my family sports were a way of life. I remember going to my brother's football games and all-star basketball games and wanting to be just like him. I used to beg my parents to let me play football like my cool older brother. Sports were my relief. On a bad day, a court or a field could change everything. When I was younger and my brother was still home he would take me outside and we would shoot hoops for hours and no matter what problem I was facing it would disappear. I have always had such a passion for the sports I have played and truly believe they will always give back in a time of need. Seeing my high school support me years after I had taken off that Bulldog uniform was beyond words. I learned to fight on those courts. It was truly an honor to be carried out there again on those girls' backs.

Another Day of Kryptonite Behind Me...
02/02/2012

My brain won't stop right now. Typical! Today was treatment day and besides the nausea I don't feel too bad. But the day of treatment is never that terrible. On the plus side they only poked me once today to get my IV! I am going to try some vitamins to help with my blood count so I can get a port. Life will be easier once I have that.

So, as I was sitting through chemo today, it got a little rough. I was feeling really sick, but started to remember everyone who had reached out to me. Whether it had been an email with a little inspiration in the form of a four year old, (hi Ava!), a message on Facebook, or a card in the mail, it all helped me get through today. Thank you all.

It is such a mental game walking into the Clinic. How can a place that will help you be so terrifying? But a lot of things in life are mental; it's all about how you handle those things that will determine how you will get through it. I have chosen this path of speaking out against my cancer, but let little situations like a low blood count and no port defeat me. That isn't ok. I need to focus on what I've done so far; a response that stuck out to me was when I was called superman, and told that chemo was my kryptonite. While I'm not sure that I am or will ever be anyone's hero, the kryptonite part really struck me. It was my kryptonite. It's going to break me down and make me weak, but when I get far enough away from it, just wait and see how strong I am! I plan on taking on every fear I have ever had, and making the moves I've been too nervous to make, because life is too short to live in fear of pain, weakness, and heartbreak. I may be sick, but I am still me, I still laugh at everything, make bad jokes, and get really mad when I watch someone play bad defense. I even still have my hair! While I don't see that lasting, I will still be me without it.

I surprised my team the other day and showed up in Slippery Rock. I was sporting a mask, which I wasn't happy about, but I wanted to see them. I was able to go to a practice, that's why I mentioned bad defense! Hopefully they are just shaking the rust off from winter break, but they hurt me more then chemo! (Love you girls! Just jealous my playing days are over). It was great being back and I think on my good weeks I will try it more often. The plan all along had been to not let this thing hold me back. I just need to get back to it now. It won't be easy and it may even get scary, but why live life going through the motions?

With another treatment behind me, spirits up, faith strong, body moving.

I'm Not lucky, I'm Blessed
02/06/2012

Last week, when I was getting my blood work done, I was talking to the nurse about my cancer. I assumed she just knew why she was taking my blood, but she actually had no idea. She was telling me how amazing I look, how my hair looks great, my skin looks great, and I just look healthy. When I thanked her I said, "Yeah, I have been really lucky." She looked at me and said, "Oh no, honey, don't call it luck, you've been blessed."

She was right. I have been blessed. Throughout all aspects of this terrible situation, I have been blessed. I have an incredible family, a support system beyond anyone's belief, and I have strength. This last treatment didn't knock me down like it could've. This whole time I've been told that typically, it gets worse, and there is still a lot of time left for that to happen. But for now, I'm counting my blessings. I still have my complaints, don't get me wrong, cancer is no walk in the park! But when I complain, I feel a little guilty. I always say over and over again in my blog that somewhere, someone has it worse. But it's the truth! So, what if I'm tired? My joints hurt pretty bad, no big deal, I was a college athlete, and I could barely walk at times in my career! My chest burns, but that's just the medicine. My complaints are nothing! I hate complaining, and while I usually only burden my parents with my complaints, I'm still not a fan.

Lately, I have noticed my head is a little foggy. I don't remember details about things and I just feel weird. I have heard that it is, "chemo brain." I'm not worried about it because eventually everything clears up; it's just weird. And while physically I am feeling decent, I keep worrying about my scans. I don't know if you have had PET scans before, but the dye they inject always makes me feel terrible. I am not looking forward to that and even more so, I am freaking out thinking that the chemo isn't working. I know it's dumb and I know it is working. Especially since I can feel that the lump in my neck is gone; it's just scary. To go through this hell every other week is not fun and to think about having to do more of it. No Thanks! My mother made me start new vitamins today. One literally looked like baby poop, and while she gags as she pours it into an alligator—yes alligator—medicine cup, she expects me to just take it like a champ! It was terrible looking and she is cracking up, loving every second of it! That woman, I swear! For the record, it tastes as bad as it looks.

I saw the Eli Manning commercial for Disney World today; you know the one that says, "You just won the Super Bowl, what will you do next?" Well, I'm looking for someone to shoot my commercial for when I beat cancer and say, "I'm going to the Wizarding World of Harry Potter!" There's a slight possibility that I am twenty-two going on twelve.

Anyways, my head's up, so whatever life is currently throwing at you, remember to stand tall, be proud, and don't let anything knock you down. You're stronger than you think!

Surgery, Stewart's, and Balding
02/10/2012

I have a port! I couldn't be happier, that sounds so weird, but I was literally more pumped for surgery than I have been for anything lately. This means fewer needles, less pain, and shorter chemo! Surgery was yesterday morning and I am pretty sore still. I have to keep the bandages on until Sunday, so I am not sure what I am working with yet, but I am so thankful for it.

The surgery was pretty interesting. They didn't put me under; they just gave me medicine to relax me, so I slept through most of it, but then I woke up while they were nearing the end. I was talking to them about what they were doing, and asking about my bandages. Pretty weird huh? I have crazy things taking place in my chest and in an artery and I'm just chattin' it up! Not much surprises me anymore.

Today I went to Stewart's Caring Place for the first time. It's an incredible place for cancer patients and their caregivers. There are exercise classes, massages, support groups, and all kinds of other awesome classes. And everything is *free*! I went to a class called Look Good, Feel Better, today. It's a make up class to teach you how to deal with the skin changes from chemo and just how to make yourself feel and look as healthy as before. It's incredible, they give you so much make up! I got tons of Mary Kay products and had to be the model for how to wear scarves and hats, even though I still have my hair. Usually, you can bring anyone with you to the sessions. Since this was my first time going I asked my mom to come. Unfortunately when we got there, a rule had changed with this session and she wasn't allowed in. I was fine at first, but when I looked around and everyone looked, at the very least, twice my age, I started to get really upset. It was hard to be out of my comfort zone without my support system, and thinking about how bad it sucks to be twenty-two with this disease. But as always, I thought about how I am not the youngest and I am not the only one, so I stuck around. On a selfish note, sometimes I think this is ok. I mean, I am twenty-two and battling something incredible. Think about how my outlook on life will change after this. And on the other hand, I think this is not fair at all. I haven't even gotten to experience life. I mean, yeah, I have done the whole college thing, but it's not like I got away from it for long. I can be selfish occasionally, and I know that, but I am not a fan. People have it worse than I do.

You know what has been killing me lately? (And if I offend you, I can honestly say I am NOT sorry,) every time I see someone smoke a cigarette! All I can think is, "Seriously, light up again and volunteer yourself for cancer one more time, because I have never smoked a day in my life and I got it! How stupid can you be?" You think quitting smoking is hard? Try chemo. Good Luck!

I don't think my hair will be around for much longer. It's starting to fall pretty quick now, and I am noticing some bald spots. It's hard, but I'll deal. Just another stupid part of cancer to stand up to. I'll get through it, I'll be me, and maybe I'll even have a Mohawk for a day when it's time to shave it. Just so it doesn't seem like I am sugarcoating things to seem like Super Woman, this never gets easier. The emotions, the treatments, the changes, it's hard all the time. Some days are easier to deal with, but there's never a break. It is the hardest thing I have ever challenged myself with. But, I think I am doing an ok job.

I just want to do more with my cancer. I want to beat it, but I want to make it suffer. I want to help people so much, that cancer doesn't stand a chance again. I just want to make what I am doing matter and be bigger.

―――

The distraction of helping others and striving to do more with my battle saved me. Just writing alone helped me clear my head. A lot of patients look into therapy, I used my writing and drawing. Whatever it is that can keep you sane in times of struggle, do it. Anything that can help you clear your mind is well worth it in these situations.

Greatness
02/22/2012

Well, if I am not the flakiest blogger, I am not sure who is! I should probably be more careful with time between blogs. All you out-of-towners assume the worst! The simple truth is, I just haven't felt well and didn't want to spend my time at a computer. Lame, I know but I am the one who is sick here, so back off already! ;)

I guess I will start with letting you all know that my port was an extreme success. I only have to endure three hours of chemo and only one needle! It's so weird, when I think about chemo or the clinic; I literally get sick to my stomach. So, the only other thing I will say about that is that I have been sleeping a lot and feeling pretty nauseous.

A lot had been going on besides how I have been feeling. Stow boys basketball team held a free throw shoot-a-thon, where they took pledges for 100 free throws and the proceeds will go towards my medical bills. My parents and I went to watch when the event took place and it was pretty crazy. All the support was still overwhelming. It was greatly appreciated and difficult to see. I am fighting this battle every day, but seeing lime green bracelets and t-shirts and banners and flyers with my name on it, still just makes this so much more real to me. I can't tell you how weird it was to walk into the high school and see my face on the doors, and yesterday in the commons there was a poster with my name on it for bracelets being sold! It's nuts! But the guys were all pretty amazing and the coaching staff was incredible. I told the boys the only reason I didn't shoot with them was because I didn't want a cancer patient to out shoot them. I think I caught them off guard! Last night, I went to their game, and once again seeing all the support was overwhelming. The cheerleaders were wearing their lime green shirts and I had to speak to the whole gym on a mic at half time! Didn't see that coming.

I am not sure if I mentioned a while ago that the girl's team held a game in my honor. That was a whole new level of weird because I remember most of those girls from when they were little and I was coaching them at camp. I went to see them today at their practice and thanked them for what they did and wished them luck in tournaments.

I am a believer in wishful thinking, fate, destiny, and more recently I am a believer that everyone has some greatness within them. I don't think many people see that in themselves or in others and I think it is a shame. Whether someone is a great friend or a great athlete or a great student, whatever it is, I think their greatness should be recognized. So, to all of my supporters, and even more so to all of those fighting for *something*, I am recognizing your greatness. You can do and be whatever or whomever you want, it's never too late to start living. It may be a hard battle getting there, but with a little faith and a lot of hard work anything is possible. Tell someone they are great today, and let someone tell you the same. Quit questioning why people are nice, question meanness and hatred instead. This world and this life can be incredible, but only if we let it. Throughout my battle, I have made many promises to myself, being great at everything I do is one of those. Not in a way that failure isn't an option, because failure is a part of experience and learning, but just in a way that whatever I do I will give it my all. Even when I am scared or in pain I'm fighting this disease, and if I can do that, I'll be able to fight through anything in my life. And through it all, I will remind myself that I am strong, and that I have greatness within me. And so do you. Believe it, find it, and keep it. Life is too short to live it half way. Fight for the best and be proud of what you achieve.

I promise it won't be this long before another blog… sorry to abandon everyone.

So Happy
03/01/2012

Ding Dong, the cancer's dead! Received news today that the cancer was no longer active and that all of my tumors have shrunk! I will be done in June, just in time to return to summer camp. After camp, *Wizarding World of Harry Potter*! It's been a very good day for my family and I. I couldn't be happier with the news, but I am well aware of the fact that I still have a tough road of chemo ahead of me. But, *Still I Rise, Still I fight*!

I have been extremely blessed throughout this entire process, and I sincerely thank all of *you* for that. Your prayers, kind words, and support have meant more to me than you will ever know. You have given me something to fight for that some people don't get. There have been times when I wanted to quit more than anything. But I couldn't let every one down. I couldn't let down my family, my friends, the campers who I promised I would return to camp, and I certainly couldn't let down the people who have followed me through this journey from the start. Today, I was thinking about the phone calls I made to friends when

I was diagnosed, some of them were camp friends, where I had to start with, "Listen, don't freak out, but I have to tell you…" All because I was afraid she was going to have a heart attack. Some were friends that I was inseparable from in high school, which I really hadn't talked to for awhile, but I always knew she'd be around. Hearing her cry on the phone broke my heart. And other big conversations for me included my team and my old roommate. I was more worried about half of them than I was about myself! But, honestly I think the distraction had kept me sane. I know what friends have been through cancer with a family member, I know what friends I have to break things down for. My favorite text during the diagnosis period was from a guy friend from college…He said, "break this down for me, and it isn't in your damn knees right?!" For once, I could say no to something concerning my knees, felt nice in a weird way…

I have learned so much through this process it has been incredible. And to be honest, I wouldn't change one surgery, one needle, or one tumor that is in my body. All the pain, all the nausea, the tests, the bad times, they have taught me so much about myself. I don't know if you're aware, but I am kind of a beast! I'm kidding. But I am strong and I will never let anyone or anything try to tell me different for the rest of my life. I've always said, "I have this disease because I can handle it," and I have, and I will. I have seven more chemo appointments. Seven more. Ask my team what it feels like to have seven more laps in the timed 2.5 miles. "OMG, seven more, so close, I think I can do it, I can't do it. Yes, I can. Stop thinking, just count." I am done thinking. From now on when I start to think, I will just say "Seven…" Seven was all I need to hear and all I need to think about. And I promise you; I am going to sprint and fight the whole way there. Then I am going to go back to a place that gave me some of the best friends in the world and to enjoy a summer of celebration with those people. Then I am going to live my life. The life I have questioned and feared, and I am going to live it without the questioning and the fears. Because I have all of you and I have God. Look what this team has gotten me through. We are unstoppable!

Don't ever give up on your dreams. No matter how hard life gets or what curveball is being thrown at you. Fight through it. I am grateful for this experience at this age. That's so weird to say. But, it's the truth. Most twenty-two year olds have no clue and just live life by going through the motions. I'd never wish this experience on anyone, but I do wish this feeling of enlightenment, and pride, and belief on the entire world.

The three things I have been praying for with my disease have been continuously answered. Spirits Up. Faith Strong. Body Moving.

Seven more!

The subject of telling people was a struggle for me. Of course there was the list of obvious people I needed to tell before word had gotten out, but it's hard to break that kind of news to people you love over the phone. I remember the night I was going to tell some of my teammates like it was yesterday. While waiting for them to finish lifting that night I received a phone call from a camp friend in Seattle. That was a hard one. Then I told a group of my closest friends on the team. Their reactions were priceless. One was Googling my symptoms, one was searching her neck for lumps, and the others were just silent. After that, I told the whole team in person. Some people received phone calls, some heard it face to face, and some received messages through Facebook. I did it my way and in my own time. I wasn't a professional about it by any means. But I held myself together the best that I possibly could to convince those people that I would be fine. One of the best responses to the news was from my Camp Director's daughter. She simply said, "Is it curable?" I answered and she replied, "Oh, alright you'll be fine then I'm not worried!" Her confidence in me at that moment carried me through the whole process. With so many people believing in me, even in the hardest times, all I had to do was remind myself that I would be fine.

Sunscreen, Gallon Challenge, and My *Rocks*
03/11/2012

All this sunshine and warm weather is just terrible to deal with! Psych! I am currently in North Myrtle with my lax team and I couldn't be happier…unless, you know, I didn't have cancer!

We left Thursday night and we have had one scrimmage and a bunch of practices. I love being back near the game more than you know. Being here, I feel less like a cancer patient and more like I am living out the year I had originally planned. I was pretty nervous about the trip, and still have some anxious moments while I am here. It's hard being away from my cancer comfort zone. I am very confident that I will be perfectly fine, but there is that fear in the back of my mind of being away from my doctors and my parents. The good news is that I have twenty-nine people here to yell at me to put on my sunscreen and to hydrate. And trust me they do! Lindsay and I have a gallon challenge going on. We both have a gallon of water and whoever finishes first for the day wins. Just for the record, I am 2-0.

I miss playing so much. The worst part was that I am cleared to play from my knee surgery, but don't have the strength to do it. I am still pretty bummed about how my career ended and I am definitely jealous of all the girls playing. I don't think they realize how lucky they are to be doing what they love. I am just lucky to still be apart of it. I wish I could explain to them how much they've helped me. They have taken my approach on my cancer and run with it. They pick on me, check in on me, and some of them even tried Lola on! A few of them have my green bracelet on their sticks and all of them play with a lime green HEADstrong Shoelaces. Their support has gotten me through a lot in the past and they just continue to be a rock for me. I'd give anything to still be on the field with them, but my time is up. All I can do now is try to prepare them for their battles, while I do my best to win mine.

On more of a cancer front, I am definitely noticing my chemo brain while I am here. I had noticed it at home, but here it's a lot more obvious. I keep having moments where I just forget things. I can't recall what I wanted to tell the defense and Lindsay keeps making the mistake of asking me to remind her of something. Typically, she never gets her reminder! I am dealing with my usual chest pain, which was just the constant reminder of the fact that I am fighting cancer. It's kind of frustrating because even on my best days, I have to put up with pain. I am pretty weak at practice as well. I have a stool that the team carries around for me to sit and coach from. I am not fond of being so weak. Being that I have been an athlete my entire life, weakness is not something I am used to. But with all the laughs and good times I am having, it is easy to fight through the pain.

As always, my spirits are up, my faith is strong, and my body is slowly but surely moving! And yes, Mom and Dad, I am napping, I check my temperature regularly, I am chugging water and Gatorade, and have taken every necessary pill. I can't touch the turf without at least three people telling me to put on sunscreen and the team will constantly carry around my water jug! I am in excellent hands here, so please enjoy a cancer free week!

Fight
03/18/2012

I apologize for my sporadic blogging lately. I am finally home from spring training and have some serious mixed emotions about it. I had such a blast being with my team, Lindsay and MB. I can't even begin to explain the nonsense that occurred on this trip. There was a lot of dancing, singing, laughing and lacrosse, all of which I have missed more than anything.

As I face this opponent in my life I continue to learn more about myself and the people around me. I have been blessed with such caring and fun people who continue to support and look out for me. Watching the game of lacrosse was a hard thing for me. I am very passionate about the sport and would give anything to be on the field again. But with this week I have learned that I have such a strong passion for coaching that I will be just fine being on the sideline. Lindsay has often told me about how rewarding coaching was, to put time in a player and see them succeed. She was right. The only thing that makes it better was the fact that I already have a connection with a majority of the people I am now coaching. My team means the world to me. They have been there through some of my toughest moments in life and just continue to stick by my side. They now warm up in lime green shirts that say, "Fight Like a Girl," on the front, and the back says, "4," and, "Still we rise, still we fight." That definitely made me cry! I figured I would be emotional watching the first game because of the fact that I wasn't out there with them, but I was crying for a whole different reason. There are moments throughout this whole process, where I feel like I don't deserve to complain, or that I am not really fighting anything. I know that sounds crazy, but it's just how I feel. So seeing twenty-seven, (not a proper coaching term, but,) friends, warming up in that shirt hit me hard. I am fighting everyday. And I do have the right to complain; everyone has that right from time to time. They just gave me twenty-seven reasons to fight harder.

There was a moment on spring break where I did have a complete break down. The girls were out on the beach at night, filming a scene for their music video, yeah, they're weird. I decided to go check it out and was immediately side tracked by the sky. The stars were breath taking and reminded me of two different moments in my life. The first was camping with my family when I was little. That one got me just because I missed my family and love the memories of those trips. And the second memory was of the summer camp where I work. The sky at night there is incredible, and a lot of times I will sit on duty and just think about life while staring at the sky. As I snapped back to reality from these memories I began to cry. I missed those moments and the people involved in those moments so much, but the worst part was thinking back to a day without cancer. I only have seven more treatments, but to me that feels like a lifetime. Lindsay came over to see what I was doing and I told her about those memories. As we were talking I told her that sometimes I wish I could quit. I told her how much I hate complaining, but it's hard. I hate being weak, I hate being sick, and I just hate cancer. I told Lindsay that I would never actually quit, but I hate feeling like a burden. She of course told me how crazy I am, but most of all she just let me talk and cry. After we talked about it for a couple of minutes, she hugged me and just reassured me that I am going to beat this in no time. I am the luckiest person to have her in my life through this. She has become my big sister, and a medicine nag! But I wouldn't change her nagging for second.

There were a couple other moments on the trip that were a pretty big deal for me. One night after I got out of the shower I decided to show a bunch of the girls my balding head. When I pull my hair back it covers all my bald spots so they hadn't really seen it yet. After showing them, I pulled Lola out and let some of the girls try her on. We all had a good laugh, but for a couple of girls I could tell they didn't like it. I understand, no one likes to deal with it, but it was a huge thing for me to show so many people my balding head. On the way home from the trip I was sharing a seat with one of my closest friends. I don't remember how it came up, but I asked Morgan how she was going to handle seeing me bald. She said that it wasn't going to be easy for her, and my response was, "Why?" I told her that I have cancer now and she handles it just fine. And she said, "Because then it will be more real." And she's right. I am nervous for that day too. I think when that moment happens, this will become a whole new level of *real* for myself. That day will be one of the hardest yet.

I guess what I am trying to say is that fighting for anything is hard. Whether it's a lacrosse game, surviving school, or fighting for your health, there are always times when you want to quit. And I think that's alright. As long as in those moments of weakness you can get a grasp of a reason worth the fight. That is what my team, my family, my beliefs, and Lindsay, have continued to do for me. So, yeah, life's hard sometimes, but it's worth the fight. Fight with purpose. Fight with pride. And fight with the knowledge that someone out there is in your corner for when you fall. If you can't find them, look to me, I'll fight for you, I'll fight with you, and I'll fight when there seems to be nothing else left to do.

———

Around this time in my treatments I made a huge decision for myself. At the time of my diagnosis I had had a boyfriend on and off for almost three years. We met in college and he was one of my best friends. When I was diagnosed I told him that this was a scary thing and he didn't have to face it if he didn't want to. He said he was in. I thought that I would marry this guy. He was everything I could've dreamed of, but with the cancer becoming more real, things seemed to change.

Cancer is hard to face when it comes to seeing someone you love go through it. And it was just too difficult for him. It was hard for me to continue to go through the motions in this relationship when I didn't feel as though I was receiving the support I needed. So, I decided I wanted to end it. Part of me did think it was crazy, I was so sick, what if I were to regret it when everything was over? But then I thought about how many people were stepping up and supporting me that I never would've imagined being there. And he wasn't one of them.

To this day, I don't blame him. I will never regret a single day of our relationship, but I also wouldn't and won't allow myself to stay in a situation that isn't giving me what I deserve. People may think I wasn't in a proper mindset to decide something like this, but I believe I was in the best mindset of my life. I knew the kinds of things I wanted when my battle was over, and I knew that I was fighting like hell for them.

I didn't just break up with a boyfriend at this time; I was also starting to realize who my true friends were and who weren't so true. In a time of crisis people tend to do one of two things for a friend: step up or step out. I had an incredible amount of people step up for me. People, who I never could've imagined saving me, did. It was a struggle though; realizing someone that you had invested so much time in was letting you down when you really needed him or her. But everyone handles fear and worry in different ways. And I will not blame the situation entirely on them; I never told them I needed them. But I also didn't feel the need to. It was best for me to focus on the people I did have, and forgive, but also forget the ones who weren't completely there.

Sorry!
04/02/2012

I have a lot of updating to do. First let me explain why I haven't been blogging. I have accepted the fact that I am physically weak and exhausted all the time. I don't tend to let that stop me from doing things anymore. I just know that I need to rest every now and then. What I cannot accept is my mental weakness. I have always had a strong memory; I am insanely good with names after meeting someone once. I received extra credit in college because the second day of classes I was able to name every student in an elective class. Now, I can barely remember what I ate for breakfast! I started to notice how bad my memory was on spring break, when I'd want to tell the team something I could never remember what it was. I asked Lindsay for a notebook and pen, and then forgot the notebook and pen! This had made school extremely difficult. I don't think my parents understood how bad or frustrating this part of treatment was for me until I was trying to tell my mom a story. I must've attempted this story three times and would just forget what I was talking to her about. I became extremely frustrated and just started to cry. I hate it! I can't stand feeling like I don't have a brain. With online classes, I am pretty much teaching myself. Which is extremely difficult to do when I can't read, because I can't remember what I am reading. And I can't write a decent paper because I forget what I am talking about! I have fallen behind in classes, I am now only in one class because the professor was being extremely generous with time.

On a more positive note, I have continued to witness greatness throughout all of these struggles. Friday, my team played Millersville University. From running this site I had seen that Millersville ordered 23 Fight Like a Girl t-shirts and assumed they would be warming up in them. Even with knowing that this was happening, I began to cry as soon as Lindsay and I walked across the field. Seeing the support from my team was overwhelming enough, but from another team in the conference just blew my mind! It was so uplifting to see their support. I spoke to their coach before the game, she was so kind hearted and caring, she said her team was on board with supporting me the minute she told them what was going on. I thanked the team after the game. Saturday our team hosted a *Stick it to Cancer* game. They were raising money for the HEADstrong Foundation. Which was a lacrosse foundation for blood cancer. Shippensburg wore the lime green HEADstrong shirts, and the stands were filled with lime green. A majority of my team sported the number 4, some of them had phrases like, *Still we rise, Still we fight,* on their calves, and some had, *Fight like a Girl.* They kept saying that it was my day. To me it was just another day of my team supporting me like they have this entire battle. They give me strength everyday I am around them. They keep me laughing and keep me sane. When I am with them I forget about being sick and just have fun. Leaving Slippery Rock on Saturday night, I couldn't stop smiling. I told my mom it was a great weekend. It was one I will never forget. I was with friends and family, being supported by complete strangers and looking forward to the day I can say, "Yes, I had cancer, I beat it though."

I wish I had more time to update you all, and I will try my hardest to blog more. But right now, there is a very cute, but extremely wild puppy demanding my attention! His name is Storm and he is a cancer/early birthday present. I need to go stop him from chewing my mother's carpets. Spirits up, Faith strong, Body moving. Tomorrow's a new day…and soon *tomorrow* will be cancer free!

With my birthday nearing and treatments becoming more and more draining, my parents were determined to make my birthday incredible. I don't remember much leading up to getting my puppy, but I have heard my parents tell the story many times. According to my parents, during chemo I reacted a lot differently than I had in any past treatments. Normally, my color would drain and I would just turn incredibly pale, this treatment I went from pale to literally being green. The normal routine after treatment was that my dad would go get the car and my mom and I would wait in the clinic until he was there. Then they would give me my pillow and blanket and I would sleep on the ride home, if my pain and nausea would allow it. Apparently on this ride my mom asked me what I wanted for my birthday, and my response was, "I just want to be cancer free." As anyone can imagine this broke my parents' hearts. When we got home, I crawled into their bed on the first floor, so they could help me if I needed anything. I was feeling so horrible after this particular treatment, I didn't know what to do with myself. Then my mom came running into the room and said, "Let's go get you a puppy!" That was all it took, I was out of bed dressed, and in the car with a picture of the puppy I was going to pick up. He is the greatest gift I have ever received. He was so aware of me being sick; it was crazy. I always applied pressure to my chest when it would hurt until I fell asleep. Once I had Storm, I would wake up and he would be lying right where I was always pushing. He would walk on my chest, and if he felt my port he would move away quickly. After treatments he would always sniff my port then lay on my chest. And anytime I would cough without him near me, he would rush into the room and check on me. In the times where I was really sick and in pain, I remember hearing my dad saying that I always would brighten up when he would bring Storm to me. I think that little puppy helped all of us get through the tougher days.

Light...
04/05/2012

I am on such a high right now!…not that kinda high ;)… Today was chemo day, beginning of cycle four which would originally be my last cycle if I would've chosen the radiation route…Only 5 more treatments and for me it was the much safer decision.

Lately, everyone has been telling me how close I am to being done. It wasn't really settling to me because I didn't know when that last treatment would be. Today, I got the date. I feel like there is a light at the end of the tunnel now. Six weeks after my last treatment, I will be getting scans to see how bad I kicked this thing's ass!

That was just the start to my great day. Tonight my team played our rivals, a team who every single one of us hates. It's just how it's always been. In my four years playing, we never beat them. We had overtimes and would always battle to the end, and come up short. Last season they were the first team I was sidelined against due to my ACL and meniscus. They're the one team that I cannot stand watching the game and not being out there with my team.

Tonight my sisters killed it. They beat this team with grace, pride, and heart. And I was out there. I was on our goalies arm in permanent marker, on our scrappy little defender's calf was a number four, and the team carried me out there the minute they put on their fight like a girl shirts. They have carried me through more than anyone in the past year alone. Some of them have seen me through two knee surgeries, some of them witnessed my last knee injury and posted it to Facebook. Thanks Morgan! But every single one of these girls has carried me through the toughest battle of my life. There was no way chemo could've kept me from this game, from supporting these girls tonight, and from the pure joy in finally showing this team that we are better.

It's moments like today and tonight that make me appreciate every bump, battle, and blessing I have. Life can be hard, but we create our own happiness. That's why I keep pushing. I don't know what tomorrow holds, I don't know what my future scans will say, and I don't even know if I'll be able to stand up tomorrow after all this activity on chemo day. But what I do know is that at any given moment I have a team full of sisters to pick me up when I fall, an unbelievable family to support me in times that I may fail, and a faith in God and life that with the right attitude and enough fight anything was possible.

> Happiness is not a destination. It is a mood, it is not permanent. It comes and it goes. And if people

thought that way, then maybe people would find happiness more often

—One Tree Hill

My spirits have never been higher. My faith had never been stronger…And believe it or not my body was moving in the last four minutes of that game! I'm still not lucky, I am extremely blessed.

Fourth Quarter
05/03/2012

Do you know that moment when you have just driven yourself somewhere and you realize you don't remember anything about the drive? That's how I feel. How did I get here? One night in October, I woke up and felt a lump. I told Lindsay about it, calling myself a freak and laughing it off. Now I will be in and out of machines for the rest of my life. How the hell did I get here?

The holidays are all a blur, not a single memory sticks out, I don't remember my first chemo, I will never forget my first ER visit and how grateful I am for Lindsay, I don't remember much of lacrosse season, yet I'm laying here, pretty worn out and only three treatments away from being done with cancer. I don't remember the details, but I can say that this was a hard drive. More bumps and potholes than I ever believed could exist. But with my family and friends and all of you reading, I am nearing my destination and for the most part my car is in one piece.

That's the best metaphor for me to explain where I am. Treatments are getting harder the closer I get to the end, and more than ever before I keep telling myself, "Still I rise, Still I fight." that's the only thing left to do. Treatments make me feel horrible, and yes, they're harder, but who stops fighting in the fourth quarter? I was never the type of athlete to do that, so I refuse to be that type of cancer patient. This whole thing has been broken down like a game for me. Because sports are all I've ever known. They make sense to me and are dependable and always here for me. As long as you are mentally and physically prepared they are usually pretty good to you as well. Sometimes I am losing my mental game lately. I get really nauseous stepping foot into the clinic, which makes the start of my drugs bad. When they access my port, I seem to freak myself out right before they shove the needle in there. It's just becoming harder to keep my head. But I can do it. I only have to do it three more times!

My last treatment, I will get to ring a bell in front of all the nurses and staff. My nurse told me a whole basketball team came to watch their teammate once and that a lot of people make a huge deal about it. Unfortunately my team, who have been my Rocks (get it?) will all be scattered back to their homes. That's ok though, I told the nurse they might need a new bell, when I'm done ringing it! How simple is that though? A bell...That I am looking forward to more than anything right now. I highly recommend more focus on the little things to get you through a struggle. Everyone these days thinks they're entitled to fireworks, and all the riches in the world. Step back. You are no better than the person on either side of you. You have no entitlement; you get what you give. People seem to forget lately that you need to work for what you want. I worked my ass off to beat this disease and I want to ring that bell. There's my victory, I don't need a huge show, I just want to ring the bell. I guess, I've been thinking about that kind of stuff a lot lately with what I see all over the sports world, it's disappointing for me seeing athletes more worried about money than the sport they're playing. I had my senior season taken away from me, and my world ended. My heart was broken. Then I get cleared to play and run around with my team and I get cancer. I need to talk to the lacrosse gods because something isn't right here! I'd give anything to play, and I know I'd work hard to get it back, and eventually I will just for the heck of it. But my game wasn't completely taken away. I still have the ability to share my knowledge and passion for the sport with others and for that, especially through this little bump in the road, I am truly blessed.

Work for what you want, focus on simpler things. I'm not trying to become the next Pat Summit in the coaching world; I'm just trying to give back to a game that had saved me more times than I can count and always been there for me. You don't need fireworks and you don't need someone telling you how great you are, although I am sure you are. If you aren't happy, change it. If something isn't working out, try something else. Life is too short to create your own unhappiness.

And to all of you parents, especially mine; you all are put through the ringer so many times with us kids. We can be rude, selfish, demanding, and do stupid things, but at the end of the day you stick by and come to the games, the hospital visits, the school events, all of it. Sometimes you want to deck us, sometimes you're overcome with pride, but you love us all the time. Thank you. You're doing a great job. Not enough children say and actually realize that we wouldn't be here without you. So, in all the hard times you all face, today's blog is for you, the parents. Keep your spirits up, your faith strong, and your body moving. Remember we are going to mess up, but remember you did too! And lord, the stories I know about my mom and dad, I am an angel! ;)

I love all of you supporters! Three more y'all!!!!

YOLO
05/21/2012

YOLO, you only live once; a phrase that has been used constantly lately when you listen to a song or log on to twitter. I guess before it became ridiculously popular, I either didn't pay attention or just didn't care. The first time it sunk in for me, I actually took a picture. It was a couple of weeks before I was diagnosed. I sat down in my normal seat for class and someone had written it on my desk. So simple, it was like I almost anticipated what was ahead for me. I remember thinking that day how true the phrase was. I thought to myself, *Time to do me, face my fears, and live.* I have faced more fear in the past six months than I ever thought possible. And along the way I've made life decisions that I will always be grateful for. A few of which I probably never would've committed to if it weren't for this battle. Nothing crazy of course, just more along the lines of giving my all to reach my dreams, putting myself first, and realizing the kind of people I want in my life. I can honestly say I don't regret anything I've done in my life, and with this journey I'm not sure I ever will.

I've learned so much, for example, if I have to be bald, my head isn't that terrible for it! I was so scared to lose my hair, what twenty-two year old female wouldn't be? But I rock my baldhead. I'm proud of it! I took this thing head on and took all control of it. I hope that power is something I carry with me forever. I have realized that sometimes the fairy tale isn't what it seems. You have to take a step back and really look at a situation. But I won't give up dreaming for the fairy tale, because I know it exists. And I've become extremely aware of negativity. I don't know how many times I can say, "Somewhere, someone has it worse." There were times when I wish I could slap people across the face with that phrase! Call me rude if you want, but I'm also not biting my tongue these days either!

Life is too short to play Negative Nancy all the time. At some point you have to suck it up and deal. I consider myself lucky these days. I am battling this dumb thing and I am sick and I am tired, but I am living. I will be healthy again and my family is healthy, what more could I want? One of the crazy things with cancer is that you seem to become everyone's shrink. It's not a bad thing, but even my parents get it. Some days you just want to say, "Oh, was that all?" Obviously, I don't do that, but it's tempting.

I have a few wishes I've come up with through all of this. The first is that I sincerely wish I could fight cancer for everyone and just have it disappear. I hate cancer and hate that anyone has to fight it, but I will forever be willing to support and fight with anyone going through it. I wish I could really share what I have learned with people my age, because I am so grateful for every lesson. And I wish that everyone could realize that the world isn't that terrible of a place. You just have to make the best of it, and believe that good things and good people exist. Stop focusing on all the bad in your life and start embracing the good. I promise if you do this for even one day, you'll be so much happier!

Just a lot of rambling I guess. But two more treatments left and I'm giving it my all. Less than a month till I ring the bell, see two of the greatest people I know get married, and head off to camp. I can't wait!

All day, everyday. Still I rise, still I fight.

So Close!
05/30/2012

> Did you feel it change? I mean how many moments in life can you point to & say 'that's when it all changed'?
>
> —*One Tree Hill*

Sitting in that doctor's office and just hearing the word 'cancer' for the first time. That's when it changed for me. In that instant, without a doubt in my mind, I knew I had cancer. Without the biopsies and consults, I just knew cancer was my next battle. In that moment the room goes white, everything around you shrinks, and you can't hear anything the doctor says following that horrendous word. It's like your world just closes in on you. The only thing I could see was my mom. She was so scared; she went white and tears rushed to her eyes. Then came the post biopsy consult. It was so hard to focus on anything. I couldn't look at my dad because as he was fighting so hard to stay strong, I couldn't help but feel like I broke him. My dad, who jokes about everything, still screams at me for my defense, or these days my team's defense, from the sideline, looking lost in that room. I only had one question: Can I beat this? The rest was a blur.

I cannot believe I am sitting here six months later. I have a few new scars, a new haircut, and a new outlook on life. But right now all I can focus on was the fact that I only have two more weeks of this left, I did it.

I have an amazing friend who has stuck by my side and made ridiculous six-hour trips to come visit me on multiple occasions. She and I have had a couple of conversations about how good people never seem to catch a break. I think one of the most frequent thoughts I have on hearing people's stories, new diagnosis, or even reading what's in the news was; why do bad things happen to good people? As we have discussed this, we both decided we would much rather be good people who were dealt a bad hand, than bad people any day. I was thinking about all of this yesterday and I came up with my own theory. Maybe bad things happen to good people because they are the ones who can get through it. The good people are the ones with the support systems, in friends and family and in their faith. Maybe good people are dealt these situations by whomever they believe in, because that higher power believes in them. It's never easy, but how much do we learn from the struggles? I am not by any means saying that I approve of this occurring. I hate it. I wish bad things didn't happen to anyone. But for me, thinking about this situation in this light makes me feel better about it. I am going through this because I can handle it. My parents are going through this because they can handle it. And in the light of an extreme tragedy, at first no one will see it this way. But when the days of healing and accepting come along, maybe they too will think that someone in charge put a lot of faith into them to overcome it all. And that should make anyone feel special.

My theory may not make sense to anyone; it might only have significance to me. But tonight, I admitted a fear to my parents, a fear that after I ring this bell, I will come back in 6–8 weeks for my scans and be told that I need to do it all over again. The likelihood of this happening is low, according to my doctors, but the fear still exists. I won't let this fear become a burden. Mostly, because I know if it does happen again, it was because I can get through it.

With two more treatments left, *Still I Rise, Still I fight*. My spirits are up, my faith is strong, and my body is still moving. What more could I ask for?

———

The further into treatments I got, the harder it became, physically and mentally. I began to suffer from extreme anxiety and would have to be medicated before treatments or appointments. The chemicals would bring me down a lot more and the pain became more intolerable. Becoming comfortable was more and more difficult, and the only relief was sleeping, which was becoming harder and harder to do. I tried to remain positive and kept the countdown and for the most part I succeeded. But the pain endured throughout the final rounds of chemo was a pain I hope to never feel again.

Victory
06/10/2012

Finally, the night before my last treatment! To say I am excited was an understatement. Of course the anxiousness sets in when I'm trying to sleep. All I can think about is how the pains of tomorrow will be the last ones. It's the greatest feeling in the world. My life is so much different than it was 6 months ago, I see things now, I mean *really* see them. The sky looks different; the trees look greener and more alive, and little things that went unnoticed are now things that make me smile everyday. I am so grateful for this entire battle. Of course I didn't enjoy any of it, but the outcome is something I'll carry with me forever. An appreciation for life and the desire to be the best version of myself! That makes every bump, bruise, and pain worth it.

I have a pretty big week ahead of me. I have chemo on Monday, port removal surgery is Tuesday, then some healing time, and eventually I'll be making my way to my summer camp job. Looking forward to camp has kept me pushing through this whole thing. Having something to work towards has kept me motivated. I cannot wait to start working out again and to feel myself getting stronger. I can't wait to have my brain back. And my hair! I know all of these things will take time, but I'm pretty sure I can handle that!

I was driving around the other day and noticing my surroundings. I was just thinking about how much different things look now than they did before. I swear the sky has never looked as beautiful to me. As I was driving and processing this, my next thought was: *I really did this.* I started to cry. I was just overwhelmed by this sense of pride and victory. I beat cancer! I took this ugly situation and made it my own. I never let cancer control me. I did it! I beat the toughest opponent I hope to ever face and I did it all while being me. I laughed, I cried, and I fought like hell to finish this game. With a buzzed head and braces, I have never been more confident in myself. You want to mess with me? I dare you. I beat cancer, there's no way you can knock me down. You know, in a way I feel like a bad ass. I feel like I can take on the world and I'm ready to. I still expect some more bumps along the way, but I say bring it on.

My journey may be nearing its end, but my blog won't be. I still have a few things left to say! Listen for that bell tomorrow. I plan on ringing it pretty loud.

I am not sure I slept at all that night. So many emotions were taking over me. I was about to have the last needle of poison. I couldn't even believe it! That day at chemo I was surrounded by people I love and people who love me. I had my parents, had been surprised by my aunt and uncle, I had one of my favorite high school teachers who was like a second mom, my neighbor, a great friend from college, and I had my amazing friend Mike - Lindsay's husband - with me. That was the first chemo that I did not sleep through. I was too excited and had so many people around me. I am sure it wasn't easy for them to watch me go through treatment, but I certainly couldn't tell.

Then it was time to ring the bell. The family of a cancer patient donated the bell to the cancer center. It reads, "Ringing Out. Ring this bell three times well; its toll to clearly say, my treatment's done; this course was run and, I am on my way!" This was the moment I had been waiting for since the first day I heard someone ring the bell. I couldn't believe it had finally arrived. The moment I rang that bell was one I will never forget in my life. The support I had, the battles I endure, every struggle in this journey, were ringing out in that hallway. In that moment, I realized I could get through anything.

Keep Fighting
06/17/2012

Well, I am officially a week out of chemo treatments and I must say it is an incredible feeling to know that I don't have to get crushed by the chemicals soon! I feel like I have been blessed with so many great things lately; it's a little bit overwhelming, but I have never been in a happier state than I am these days.

I arrived at summer camp on Saturday and was greeted by incredible friends right away. So many hugs (from healthy people) and so many people saying they were happy to see me; it felt incredible. I was a little nervous at first, because I didn't know what to expect from people. I didn't think anyone would be rude or weird, but it's nerve wracking after six months of being pretty sheltered. I should've known better though, this place has some of the greatest people I've ever met. We were watching the highlight film from last summer on my first night here and I found myself getting choked up. For a couple of reasons really, but mostly due to the fact that I realized I made it. Camp was my finish line for all of it. Camp was the one thing I could tell myself to look forward to when times were hard. Of course being healthy was something to look forward to, but at times there are moments that you don't believe in those days. I have crossed my finish line. It is time for me to live my life again and I can't wait to live it to the absolute fullest.

God had blessed me with so much through this journey. I have the worlds strongest and most supportive parents, I have incredible friends who I now consider family because of their support, and I have my health! Soon I will begin to work out, I'll finish my class, I'll get back on the lacrosse field, and I'll do it all with a smile on my face and love in my heart. I wouldn't change this journey for the world.

You know, bad things may happen to good people, but in the end, with enough support and faith, you'll find the silver lining…You just have to fight like hell to get there.

Keep fighting.

Long Over Due Update
08/26/2012

Wow! It's been awhile! There is so much to catch you all up on. I guess I should start with my summer. As everyone knows I fought pretty hard in that last week of chemo in order to make it to Lindsay and Mike's wedding and to get to camp. I am so glad I was able to fight through those pains in order to have the summer I did.

My position at camp this summer was a lot different than being the lacrosse director. I struggled with it because of my chemo brain and not having the kind of time I was used to spending with the girls. My job was to manage photographers and to take and tag pictures. The first week was miserable because I couldn't remember any of the girl's names. I knew all the faces but couldn't get my brain to focus long enough to figure it out. Luckily, all the campers and staff were amazing at helping me deal with the stress. My support system there was overwhelming. My friends were incredible, as I expected, but the bigger shock were the campers themselves. There is a well-known child therapist who comes to our camp to talk to our staff about working with children. I was extremely nervous about the campers handling me being sick, so I spoke to him about how to handle it. At first when I told him my stories and my fears with the situation he just said, "Whoa." Typical reaction. Then he began to tell me how I had to let the kids run the conversation, and most importantly I couldn't lie to them. With this new knowledge, I was ready and anxious for the girls to arrive. I did not expect for their reactions to seeing me to be the way they were. My expectations were that kids would feel awkward around me and nervous. I didn't realize how sick I actually looked until I looked back at pictures, so I can't imagine what they thought. I had girls who I had hardly spoken to the summer before running up to me to tell me how beautiful I am. They kept telling me I could pull off bald, how strong I was, and that my eyebrows and hair would grow back in no time. They were incredible. Every day I had someone asking about my vitamins or if I had sunscreen on. And everyday they would tell me how fast my hair was growing. I don't think those girls will ever understand what they did for me this summer. They gave me confidence, they lifted my spirits, and they gave me a reason to stay strong and make sure that nothing was going to interfere with my summer. I don't think I can ever thank them enough.

Although I was dreading the end of camp, saying goodbye to great friends and great girls, I did have a huge event to look forward to—The Wizarding World of

Harry Potter. Remember way back in the beginning of my diagnosis when out of left field I decided that when I beat this disease I was going to see *Harry Potter*? Well, with the help of an organization called Compassion Partners that dream came true. Compassion Partners was kind of like an adult Make-A-Wish Foundation, they supply tickets to Universal's parks and also Sea World. My parents and I left for Florida on a Sunday and stayed for a week. I had my first Disney experience, then enjoyed two days of Universal, and a day at Sea World. I am still not sure why I wanted to celebrate at the Wizarding World, but it could very well be the best decision I have made in my life. At all of the parks we were given a Golden Ticket. Since I still have to be careful with being in the sun, this pass allowed us to cut the lines and wait indoors. At Universal we were treated like celebrities and taken through the back door and got straight into the attractions. So many dirty looks happened when we skipped the lines in Hogsmeade, especially at Ollivander's Wand Shop. My mom and I never really noticed the attention but my dad had mentioned that people would get angry and then point to my hat and scarf and stop. He isn't used to seeing the reaction as much as my mom and I, so it kind of bothered him. The trip was amazing and Compassion Partners really did make my dream come true.

So, I guess I should move on to where I am at today. I am struggling with this part, but I have to remind myself that this blog was to help others just as much as it is to clear my mind. So, here goes nothing! Over the summer I started to notice my anger and anxiety were pretty bad. The smallest thing can make me so completely enraged that my hands just ball up into fists. Stress makes my heart race to where I feel like I could pass out. And I am noticing that there are times when I am just not myself. I have a lot of days lately that I wake up and just feel incredible, so happy and blessed to be alive. On those days, I will walk into a store and ask everyone how they are. I feel good on those days. Other days are bad. And I didn't realize just how bad they were until my parents called me out on it. When we were at the parks, I couldn't handle the crowds. I couldn't handle people at all. Nothing infuriated me more than people smoking, and me having to breathe it in. On a side note, Smoking areas in amusement parks are like saying they are peeing areas in a pool that crap still spreads! Anyways, one day my mom and dad started telling me they notice my anger, and they have seen my fists and told me I might want to consider counseling. This, of course, enraged me. My response was, "I don't need counseling, until I start swinging." And my parents dropped the topic. But the smart people they are had planted this seed into my head. I began to notice my anger and anxiety even more. So, I went to Lindsay to talk it out. My feelings of counseling, (just for me, not others,) was that it was a weakness. In my head, I had been incredibly strong all throughout treatments, so

I can't be weak now that they are over. Of course Lindsay corrected me on that right away. And the point she kept making was, what kind of twenty-three year old could face a life-threatening situation and take it all on their own? And she's right. I am not weak for needing help in dealing with this. For the six months I was fighting, I was too distracted to wrap my head around things. And now with no distractions it was all hitting me. I can't believe what I went through and a lot of my anger comes in when stupid things go wrong. And all I can think is, "Well, what's next in my life?" or, "When the hell do I get a break?!" I don't like this version of myself, I don't like the negativity, and I sure as hell don't want breaks! I didn't fight for my life to sail through the rest of it. I can handle challenges every now and then; in fact I will embrace them. So, I have decided that I need to talk to someone who can help me work through these things. And I don't feel weak in admitting it. Actually, I feel stronger, because I can face reality and the fact that I can't get through this part alone. I will never regret any decision I made throughout my battle, but now I need to figure out how to deal with what happened.

I have my first scans since chemo on Friday, and to be quite honest, I am scared out of my mind. I am not worried that I still have that awful disease in me, although I have moments where it crosses my mind. But what cancer patient wouldn't? I think I am more scared of walking into that building again and seeing what emotions catch up to me. But I am strong. I know there is a lot of prayers headed my way. And whatever happens, I can take it. I've made it this far, just gotta keep pushing.

I could brag about the girls and my friends at my summer camp for days. And I would if you let me. They helped me get through a huge part of the healing process that some people just don't understand. It was the moment when I was finally done with the treatments, building up my strength, yet still physically looked like a cancer patient. I had a hard time looking in the mirror, but these girls saw me just as they always had. The only way I can describe how they saw me and how they supported me was by using one of their own words. One of the older campers sent me an English paper she wrote for school, the title was, "Hair is so Overrated," and the part that shows the spirit of these girls best was as follows:

> A slideshow of past camp memories flashed across my mind—but one individual stuck out among the rest. I opened my eyes and there she was, boasting the world's biggest smile upon her braced teeth. Her skin was as white as snow, her lips cracked and dull. Little stubs of hair outlined where here eyebrows used to be. A bright red bandana and a straw hat covered the few loose strands of hair left on her almost-bald head. The only thing that reinsured me it was her; the smile that still spread half way

across her face…Looking at her now, was the result of what she had gone through all year. …I sprinted toward her and pulled her fragile body towards mine. Her bones stuck out of her skin, but I did not care. I held her tightly. My hand grasped her shirt. Tears began to flood my eyes. I leaned back still holding on tightly to the cloth of her shirt. She looked into my eyes and said, "Hey bud."

The strength and confidence these girls gave me will be something I cherish forever. I could not imagine spending my first couple of months out of treatments anywhere else. They are the reason that camp was always something I fought for. I realize how incredibly difficult it must have been for the owners to allow me to come back fresh out of chemo, but I am not sure I would have built up the confidence anywhere else.

For the Last Time...
09/16/2012

As most of you already know, I survived my first post-treatment scans. Not only did I survive them, I have been told I am in remission. The day started with a lot of nerves and anxiety, but as always, I had my parents by my side. Showing up at the cancer center was by far the worst part of the experience. It was like everything I have tried to block out came rushing back to me, it was scary. A lot of random memories would pop up and seeing the people fighting not only broke my heart but made me a little nauseous as well.

The day first started with some blood work. At this point needles don't hurt me anymore, I honestly don't even feel them. The only bad part was the anxiety. I know that it won't hurt, but like I said the memories that come are enough to scare anyone. After the blood work we headed over to start my scans. For the PET and CAT scans, you have to drink some fluids and be injected with a contrast dye. I hate both of these things. During treatment the fluids made me puke pretty bad, which was when they decided to tell me that they make a "kids" version that tastes like lemonade. So, naturally I asked for that right off the bat. You have to drink this fluid every fifteen minutes, and I think it ended up being four cups worth. Which doesn't sound too bad, but trust me it was. I don't think I'll be going near lemonade until the next set of scans! But the worst part comes when you are actually in the machine. Once the scans are happening, they hook you up to an IV that will inject contrast for better images. When the contrast is injected, your entire body gets warm and you feel as if you've peed yourself, not a great sensation. This part always makes me feel a little sick, and the technician remembered me from my last scans so she put a puke bucket on my stomach, which was funny because using it while in that little tube would be impossible. I don't know if you've ever seen one of those machines before but there wasn't really a lot of room for movement. They do make open machines for 'larger' people—I asked. Anyways, I was fine throughout the scans, and next we were headed to meet up with my oncologist. Luckily the place was pretty empty, so I didn't really have to see too many patients. To explain why this matters to me is simply because I hate seeing people having to go through what I did. I would gladly take their place because I hate cancer and don't want anyone to suffer through it. I know a handful of people who will read this and say that I am done and shouldn't take more, but I would chose me over anyone else; it's just my style.

Waiting for the oncologist was difficult. First of all, he wasn't my usual oncologist because mine moved to Vegas.

Second, he was an hour behind! I told you all about my mental stability in the last blog, please picture me waiting in a room for an hour to be told whether I am in the clear or not! At least I had my parents entertained. When the doctor finally arrived, the first thing out of his mouth was, "You are in remission!" That was all I needed. I could breathe again, could relax, and finally turn the page on this chapter. But then he said that there were gray areas in my scans. This was unsettling. I don't know what color scans are but I know gray doesn't mean things are where they need to be. He went on to explain that there are a few areas that still lit up in my scans. He didn't say they were particularly active, but they also weren't clear of the cancer. He said that they were areas we will watch in future scans and to listen to my body to see if anything sparks up. I went from this extreme high of being told I am in the clear to this sense of disappointment. It was like a blow to the ego, I fought most of it off, but now I have to live with gray? And in my mind was, *If this is 'gray' how is that remission?* But apparently the spots aren't big enough or active enough to need any treatment or attention. It's still pretty unsettling to me.

That is why as excited as I am to be in remission, and don't get me wrong, I'm ecstatic, I am always going to have a little bit of fear until this gray area goes away. I am sure even without having the couple of spots I would still be fearful for future scans. What is keeping me moving forward is my faith, my family and friends, and that fact that I know in time everything will be alright. Fear isn't always a bad thing. It will keep me conscious of what is happening with my body. It will keep me pushing to be healthy. And most of all, it will just remind me to love my life.

Every day is a gift. And every time there is a small bump in the road, I think about the hell that was my life for the past year. If I can survive that, I can do anything. And so can all of you. You just have to get through the bad to experience all the good.

I'm thinking this will be my last blog. It is time for me to put these pieces together and move on. I have recently gotten a new tattoo that I wear with extreme pride. It is the date of my diagnosis and "Still I Rise. Still I Fight," right under the scar where I found my cancer. I wear all my scars with pride; they are my physical proof and reminder that I can handle anything. I am starting to feel more like myself again, getting back on the lax field just for the heck of it, and trying to finish up my master's degree, which is still proving to be a little difficult on the brain. I am planning on getting extensions soon; I have seen some pretty awesome results for cancer patients. And as much as everyone says I rock the short hair, I am just kind of over it. I want to be me again. Not that hair really makes me who I am, but it's what I want so don't fight me on this one.

I will never be able to thank everyone enough for the support you have given, not only to me, but also to my family. I truly and honestly wouldn't have gotten through this journey the way I did without all of you. This experience had made me stronger, but more importantly has shown me that great people still do exist. You might not see that when you turn on the news or you read the newspaper, but please consider me living proof of that statement. I wish nothing but the best for all of you. And I sincerely hope you have all gotten as much out of reading my blog as I have in writing it. My final advice would just be a combination of all the past blogs. Live life day by day, believe in your greatness, create your own happiness, remember somewhere someone is going through worse, and finally I would just say embrace life and all it has to offer. After you read this, do me a favor and look outside, appreciate the trees and the sky and everything this world has to offer. It's an incredible place and I fought like hell to be here. But, hey, what do I know? I'm only twenty-three, and it was only cancer…;)

For the last time, keep your spirits up, your faith strong, and your body moving. And no matter what obstacle you face, just remember, "Still I rise, still I fight."

Thank you all from the bottom of my heart,
Brianne Dishong

―――

And there was the end of my story, yeah right! Life continues to be a whirlwind of emotions for me. One day I wake up and I am in love with everything, and everyone I see. The sky is a different color, the trees are a little bit greener, and the birds sing more beautifully than ever. Then I have days when I look in the mirror and see my short hair and just hate everything about that day. I just want to go back to bed and wake up with long hair and all my strength.

A struggle of mine is the thought, and at times realizations, that people think since I beat it, I am all done, and life is back to normal. This is hard for me. I am not one who wants people to fear, pity, or worry about me. But my fight is not over. Yes, the hard part is behind me, thank goodness, but every day there is a battle. Trying to wrap my head around what happened to me is a constant struggle. If I smell or taste anything that reminds me of chemo, I am instantly sent into a panic attack. And every ache, pain, or moment of fatigue sparks a small memory and ignites fear of the cancer returning.

Everyone tells me that accepting the journey will be easier, and that the anxieties will go away. I know that they are right, but it was the in between that was difficult. I struggle every day with worry, fear, and although I don't want to admit it, depression. I have felt weaker in the post-cancer days than I felt through my entire battle. But when you sit down and think about it, it makes sense. When I was fighting, all I had time to think about was surviving. I literally slept for six months of my life. Now when things are starting to fall back into place, I have time to think about what actually happened to me. None of it was fair. None of it was expected. But that's life. A year ago, I was starting treatments and I just now had the first major breakdown to both of my parents about how I am feeling. I can honestly say it was long overdue. I was so afraid to scare them or upset them that I blocked out my biggest support system. It's so important to realize that whatever you may be dealing with, you can't always get through it on your own. Crying and breaking down is not a sign of weakness. It takes extreme strength to break down and let people in, and in the end that strength will save you. Don't try to be your own hero all the time, don't try to pretend it will all go away on it's own, and most of all don't be afraid to ask those around you for help.

These feelings are normal, but hard to live with. I want to be able to get past it all and move on with my life. I will get there. One day at a time, I will get stronger, become more accepting, and soon it will just be another chapter in my life. I don't want to forget my fight; I just want to be able to understand it a little bit more. I will never close the book on this battle; I will simply turn the page.

With my spirits up, my faith strong, and my body moving, STILL I RISE, STILL I FIGHT.

Bri's Quick Chemo Survival Guide

Now I am no expert on the topic, but here are a few tricks I used to get me through:

— EAT! Even if you don't have an appetite, try to eat! It helped me stay strong during treatments and truly cut my nausea down.

— Don't forget the gum trick. Chewing gum during flushes and parts of treatments masks the chemical taste.

— Salt water gargle. If you start to develop mouth sores this was a great option if you haven't been prescribed "magic mouthwash."

— Avoid your favorite foods, perfumes, and even outfits on chemo day. You will become so sensitive to smells and tastes associated with chemo, it will be awhile before you can be around them again. Five months later and I still have a hoodie I can't wear!

— HYDRATE! Seriously, this is important! Lack of hydration will send you straight to the emergency room, and trust me it is the worst feeling in the world. You will get sick of water all the time, mix in some Gatorade or lemon.

— Take advantage of cancer centers. It's hard to find places where you feel like people aren't staring; cancer centers provide a place where everyone knows what you're going through.

— Don't be afraid to tell people exactly how you feel. If you need to be alone, say it! If you need someone around, tell them. Hell, if you just need your mom to hold you for a minute, ask her!

— Now here is a wild one: try marijuana. It will definitely help with the appetite, anxiety, and some of the pain. You will need the help.

— Find a healthy release. Whether you write, draw, sing, anything, stick to it. Keep your sanity by doing something you love, and don't be afraid to seek professional help. It's not something you can face on your own.

— Have little benchmarks and treats for yourself. I would get massages, or plan visits with people, and planned a vacation with the help of Compassion Partners.

— Remember you aren't alone. In all forms of that statement, remember you have people to turn to. Whether it's other fighters, survivors, family, or friends, you are never alone in your journey.

— Find what works for you and stick to it. Don't let anyone tell you that you are doing it wrong. It is cancer. There is no right way to go about it. Look forward to the little things and ask for help along the way. Know that there are millions of survivors that are supporting you and I am definitely one of them.

— Most importantly, know your body! It is so simple. Don't ignore something abnormal and don't only look at those breast cancer awareness signs and think that's the only cancer out there! Unfortunately, there are many. So know your body and don't be afraid to ask a doctor when something feels off. No matter how old you are this can be the key to saving your life.

For pictures and more information on my journey please visit, www.thatgirlwithcancer.com

Out of suffering have emerged the strongest souls;
the most massive characters are seared with scars.

—Kahlil Gibran